Romans
The Reign of Grace

In the Message of the Cross

Dr. Gordon E. Johnson and his wife, Grace, arrived from Winnipeg, Manitoba, Canada, for missionary service at the Rio Grande Bible Institute in 1954. He has served as Professor from 1954 to the present, Academic Dean (1968-1981) and President (1981-1995). Currently he is President Emeritus.

He graduated from Prairie Bible Institute High School (1946) and Bible Institute (1949), and from the Winnipeg College of Theology with a B. R. E (1951). His studies include: University of Texas Pan American B.A with highest honors (1965), University of Texas Austin M.A. in Latin American Studies (1970) and Trinity Evangelical Divinity School, Doctor of Missiology (1985) Deerfield, Illinois.

Romans, the Reign of Grace

In the Message of the Cross

Gordon E. Johnson

Rio Grande Bible Institute, Edinburg, Texas 78539
ISBN 978-1-4675-8346-6

Editorial Rio Grande

Published by Editorial Rio Grande
4300 S. U.S. Highway 281
Edinburg, Texas 78539

ISBN

ISBN 978-1-4675-8346-6

9 781467 583466

All Scripture references are from the New King James Version

Contents

Index

Dedication

With profound gratitude to God for the high honor
and privilege that I have,
I dedicate this expository study in Romans
to the memory of my mentor,

Rev. L.E. Maxwell
(1895-1984)

Co-founder, Author and longtime Principal of
Prairie Bible Institute
Three Hills, Alberta, Canada

As one of thousands of his students, I owe a debt of gratitude to God that I can never repay for his life, example and powerful teaching. From my early high school days, Mr. Maxwell as we called him, impacted my life, challenged my mind and heart to follow his example of being a disciplined, dedicated and faithful soldier of the Cross.

His knowledge of the Word of God, his commitment to its authority, his giftedness in interpreting it and his God-given skill in preaching molded my life and calling for a lifelong missionary service in teaching the truths of the Message of the Cross.

In a special way, through his family life, personal friendship and daily example for seven years, his greatest gift to me was his insight into our death to sin, our union with Christ as Paul sets it forth in Romans 1-8. This life-transforming truth has been my passion to teach and live before my Hispanic students and colleagues.

Leslie Earl Maxwell

A tribute to Rev. L. E. Maxwell

My dear father, Leslie Earl Maxwell, was born in 1895 in Mentor, Kansas. He grew up in a non-Christian home, the eldest of 9 children. His godly aunt Christina prayed for him for 20 years and encouraged him to attend church with her. Week after week the pastor kept saying, "Come to Christ and the church." One night under the conviction of the Spirit, he fell to his knees and cried out, "O God, forgive my sins!" The peace of God flooded his heart. That same night, he began to devour the Word of God.

However, after his conversion, he struggled with a lack of spiritual victory. He read tracts that set forth how to have victory over his sinful nature, "the Old Man" of Romans 6:11. The summer after his discharge from the army, he agonized so intensely over his sinfulness that he lost 15 pounds of body weight. That fall he enrolled in the Midland Bible Institute in Kansas City, KS. There, during a very humbling personal crisis, he discovered Galatians 2:20, "I am crucified with Christ: nevertheless I live; yet not I, but Christ liveth in me; and the life which I now live in the flesh I live by the faith of the Son of God, who loved me and gave Himself for me." This became his life verse, and identification with Christ in His death and resurrection was foundational to, and the focal point, of his entire ministry.

Daddy, as we always called him, was given an early opportunity to apply the cross in his life. He was finishing his studies at Midland when a letter arrived from Alberta, Canada. It was an invitation from a group of farmers requesting to come and teach the Bible to them and their teen-agers. Even though he did not want to serve in a cold climate, a rural setting, or do public speaking, he chose to follow Christ in not pleasing himself. His two-year initial commitment turned into a life-long ministry. So in 1922, Prairie Bible Institute was born. Mother followed him three years later, and stood valiantly by his side all his life. Words seemed inadequate in expressing his gratitude for her.

For the next 60 years Daddy impacted the lives of thousands of students with his vibrant teaching and unwavering message of the cross. Students not only observed the cross in the life of my father and the institute staff, but in turn embraced the cross and went forth to proclaim the glorious message of Christ crucified. In 2002 the Alumni Association reported that alumni were serving in 114 nations. Their influence both at home and abroad cannot be calculated in human terms. Eternity alone will reveal the results.

When it came to preaching, Daddy was manifestly anointed of God. There was a two-fold explanation for this. First, and foremost, he "let the word of Christ dwell in [him] richly" (Col. 3:16) through personal wholehearted application of it to his life. As children we observed that his mornings began on his knees, by his bed, meditating on the Word. His burning desire to follow Christ fully could be heard in the oft repeated "Oh, God" which still lingers in our memories.

The second reason for his powerful preaching was his careful exposition of the Word. He was clearly committed to "rightly dividing the word of truth" (2 Tim. 2:15), holding apparently contradictory truths in dynamic tension, not playing one truth off against another. He was fully persuaded that "all Scripture is given by inspiration of God" (2 Tim. 3:16) and is the inspired powerful "sword of the Spirit" (Eph. 6:17) in ministering to his listeners. For these reasons, sitting under his preaching, a person heard the voice of God through the word of God and became keenly aware of the presence of God.

Daddy's magnum opus, *Born Crucified*, sets forth the cross in the life of the believer as the key to victory over sin, self, suffering, Satan, and the world. First published by Moody Publishers in 1945, and republished in 2002 under the title *Embraced by the Cross*. The original title graces the cover of the 2010 republished version. Paul's words in Galatians undoubtedly express Daddy's heartfelt commitment, "God forbid that I should glory save in the cross of our Lord Jesus Christ, by whom the world is crucified unto me, and I unto the world" (Gal. 6:14).

An opportunity to live the crucified life presented itself to Daddy in his latter years. He lost the sight of one eye due to a detached retina. He jokingly quipped that he had become more Biblical as he was now "single-eyed." Seriously though, he embraced the cross and commented, "God permitted this that I might finish my course better than I otherwise would have."

Daddy's last public appearance took place not long before his Homecall. Dr. Stephen Olford was ministering at Prairie on this occasion. Daddy had already asked him to speak at his funeral. I pushed Daddy on to the Prairie Tabernacle platform in a wheel chair, and he greeted the audience. His voice was amazingly strong. Dr. Ted Rendall, who was leading the service, asked brother Olford to lead in a special word of prayer. He found it difficult realizing that the next time he would be so involved could be at Daddy's funeral service.

As I wheeled Daddy home, we commented that this had been the rehearsal for his memorial service. He spontaneously quipped, "This was the rehearsal without the hearse!"

He went Home to be with the Lord February 4, 1984. His memorial service was climaxed with the choir and orchestra presenting the Hallelujah Chorus -- Daddy's favorite. An observing journalist commented that this occasion was more like a celebration than a memorial service.

I will never cease to thank God for my dear father. One who lived the cross, gloried in the cross, and departed, resting in Christ and His work on the cross. This certainly explains why his life radiantly overflowed with the presence of Christ.

--Paul Maxwell, a grateful son

Chapter 1

THE REIGN OF GRACE IN THE MESSAGE OF THE CROSS

*"The thief does not come except to steal, and to kill, and to destroy. **I have come that they may have life, and that they may have it more abundantly**"* (John 10:10).

My deepest interest has always been the devotional life and service of the believer. I have devoted my life to sharing the Message of the Cross, essentially our union with Christ in death to sin and the abundant life through the Holy Spirit's ministry.

The believer must daily count on his union with Christ at the Cross and on that basis feed on the Word of God. A devotional study, as I propose to present in this book, has its basis solely in the inspired text accompanied by the believer's prayer that the Spirit of Christ will apply the truth to one's everyday living. Such a walk of faith leads to a transformed life, THE REIGN OF GRACE.

THE REIGN OF GRACE will not be an exegetical treatment per se, but will rather seek to establish a sound Biblical and theological basis for Paul's profound argument; his masterful development of the Message of the Cross will then become the very foundation of a victorious Christian life. Romans expresses the very essence of his message, the believer's union with Christ; in his other letters he applies those very same truths to believers in Galatia, Corinth, Ephesus, Colosse, Philippi and to his fellow workers.

Paul's presentation calls for a strong emphasis on the personal application of these truths to our daily life. Christian victory is not an intellectual argument or theoretical knowledge, but rather a real humbling and embracing of the truths of the Cross as the Holy Spirit makes them real in everyday life. Especially in Romans 5-8, these truths become a progressive walk of faith and an obedience resulting in Christ-like maturity.

The Epistle of Paul to the Romans was recognized unanimously by the early church as inspired Scripture. It was no coincidence that in the formation of the Sacred Canon, Romans was placed immediately after the Gospels and the Acts of the Holy Spirit. It was a primer for doctrine and practice. Unfortunately other teachings have displaced, sometimes, its supremacy. I trust that this study will call us back to the foundation of our faith, a Christ-centered walk and Cross-centered message.

Occasion of the Epistle to the Romans

Paul, as the Apostle to the Gentiles, had covered much of Asia and the eastern half of what was then Europe (the Greek peninsula). With missionary vision his eyes were set on a visit to Spain. *"And so I have made it my aim to preach the gospel, not where Christ was named, lest I should build on another man's foundation, but as it is written: 'To whom He was not announced, they shall see; and those who have not heard shall understand"* (15:20,21). Such was Paul's missionary heart. When studying Romans we must keep the perspective of a missionary who writes from his heart to others committed to the spreading of the same gospel.

In his letter to Rome Paul was counting on a trip to Jerusalem to *"minister to the saints"* in their poverty (15: 25). After completing this service, he would pass through Rome, the very heart of the Roman Empire, on his missionary trip to Spain. In retrospect, Paul visited Rome and there was martyred for his faith. We have no record of his trip to Spain. God had other plans for Paul.

The book of Romans is, in one sense, Paul's letter of introduction of himself as an Apostle of Jesus Christ. He introduces himself by defining, defending and declaring the gospel in a hitherto inimitable manner. The truths of Romans have challenged the greatest minds and have never been fully plumbed in centuries of godly exposition. May God illumine our hearts!

A Masterful Introduction   Romans 1:1-7

How should one approach such a challenge: a converted Pharisee who claims to be the Apostle to the Gentiles, whose reputation was both excellent and doubtful depending on who speaks? Paul's response is straight forward and direct. * *"Paul, a servant* [slave] *of Jesus Christ"* (1:1).

Rome well knew the role of the slave, an entity to be sold, bartered and used at the will of the owner. The slave brought nothing to the owner except total availability and implicit obedience. This was Paul's boast. *"Nothing in my hand I bring, simply to thy cross I cling"*; so says the well-known hymn. A slave had no rights, no station in life; he lived for his master. Paul's boast is that he is all of that, and voluntarily so.

Immediately after the giving of the Decalogue in Exodus 20, God dealt with the reality of slavery among his chosen people. In God's provision slavery could never be tolerated as a lifelong servitude. So he set a six year limit: *"If you buy a Hebrew servant, he shall serve six years; and in the seventh he shall go out free and pay nothing"* (Exodus 21:2).

However, now comes the exemption: *"But if the servant plainly says, 'I love my master, my wife, and my children; I will not go out free,' then the master shall bring him to the judges. He shall also bring him to the door, or to the doorpost, and his master shall pierce his ear with an awl; and he shall serve him forever"* (vv. 5, 6). What a beautiful picture! Notice that he first loves his master, not his wife and children. His master pierces his ear publicly. He no longer has an ear for anyone else. He is exclusively bound to obey his master and all because he plainly said: **I love my master**.

Paul's lifelong service in missions exemplifies the spirit of Old Testament slavery. What a challenge for New Testament believers!

"Called to be an apostle." But there is a dignity to this slave, conferred on him by his being a sent one, a missionary, an ambassador. Heaven, no less, has given him that charge and under divine orders he will carry it out. William Carey, the founder of modern missions (1798) said of his son: "I hope he will never stoop to be the King's ambassador to India."

"Separated unto the gospel of God." But there is more. He has been set apart, sanctified for the express purpose of proclaiming the ultimate good news of God to a dying and rebellious world. He joins the sacred ranks of prophets, priests and kings. Implicit is an anointing to be the expression of God's voice and heart.

This is no mean calling. Missionaries will not be judged by numbers, fame and success. My rich and successful brother once asked my mother: "What is Gordon doing down there in that small Bible Institute?" Just before he died as a believer, he called me and simply said: "Gordon, you chose better than I did."

Along with Paul's being separated unto the gospel, he will make much of the believer's being separated unto the Gospel in holy living. More than half of the section Romans 1-8 is devoted to sanctification, showing the vital importance of personal holiness. The forte of Paul is his step by step argument as he leads us out of self and into Christ. We must see the earlier chapters as the sure foundation of the believer's walk of faith.

The Heart of the Good News

Now comes the focus, not on Paul but on **Jesus Christ**. The Old Testament Scriptures revolved around Christ. The two discouraged disciples on the road to Emmaus heard our Lord himself expound on his death and resurrection: *"O foolish ones, and slow of heart to believe in all that the prophets have spoken! Ought not the Christ to have suffered these things and to enter into His glory? And beginning at Moses and all the Prophets, He expounded to them in all the Scriptures the things concerning Himself"* (Luke 24:25-27).

For Paul there is an overwhelming continuity between the Old and New. There may be some dispensational differences, but they are minor in comparison with the flow of grace and truth. *"For the law was given through Moses, but grace and truth came through Jesus Christ"* (John 1: 17).

This good news, embodied in the gospel, arises from the Old Testament Scriptures. Paul's New Testament salvation is no novelty. Paul is but another link in the ongoing divine inspiration. And that message revolves around the person of Christ, the Messiah. *"Concerning His Son Jesus Christ our Lord who was born of the seed of David according to the flesh" (v.3).

The **humanity** of Jesus is highlighted because he became man and accomplished the good news through his incarnation. "Inasmuch then as the children have partaken of flesh and blood, He Himself likewise shared in the same, that through death He might destroy ["katargeo"- annul] him who had the power of death, that is, the devil, and release those who through fear of death were all their lifetime subject to bondage" (Hebrews 1:14,15).

Equal emphasis is given to his absolute **deity.** *"And declared to be the Son of God with power, according to the Spirit of holiness, by the resurrection from the dead" (v.4). The **deity** of Jesus is further verified by his vicarious death followed by God's most evident vindication; he raised him from the dead. There could be no more convincing proof than that historical fact; he always was and is the Son of God.

Paul makes it clear that this was done "according to the Spirit of holiness"; that significant statement will highlight Roman's theme of God's holiness leading to nothing less than our holiness. Salvation must issue in practical conformity to Christ; the Holy Spirit is absolutely the agent of the same.

Today's preaching seems to center often more on what we as believers must do. But God has a radically different concept of salvation. As any coin must have two faces of equal value, so the gospel of grace has two complementary sides: 1) Christ died in our place, our substitute, and he declares us righteous in his sight; 2) But at the same time we died in him at the Cross, co-crucified, our old man judged (Romans 6:1-6; Galatians 2:20). Now in grace we believe and accept that fact of what he did as the very ground of our victory.

This gospel has been entrusted to us. From the mystery of his being the God-man, the one mediator from whom we *"have received grace and apostleship for **obedience to the faith among all nations** for His name"* (v.5), this becomes our mandate. Note the phrase "we have received grace and apostleship." Never can there be merit of pride or achievement. What is done is God's doing first and finally.

Paul marks the end result: a missionary purpose to all nations. It is no coincidence that the phrase *obedience to faith among all nations* is mentioned here and in the final doxology. *"Now to Him who is able to establish you according to my gospel and the preaching of Jesus Christ, according to the revelation of the mystery which was kept secret since the world began but now has been made manifest, by the prophetic Scriptures has been made known **to all nations,** according to the commandment of the everlasting God, for **obedience to the faith**--to God, alone wise, be glory through Jesus Christ forever. Amen"* (16:25-27).

Paul's overriding passion is a faith that obeys, and it is always a missionary faith that obeys. May this truth never be lost in the exposition of Romans.

He sums up the introduction by calling all such: saints, holy ones, set apart to live an abundant life in Christ. He will lay out for them and us the obstacles of sins (Romans 1:18-3:20), the "how" of cleansing by his blood (3:21-4:25) and judgment of the sin principle and the faith-walk in victory over sin by the power of the Holy Spirit (5:1-8:39). This is the glorious heritage of the saint.

In few words Paul has introduced himself as an apostle of a Christ-centered Biblical message. To this message he is utterly committed: *"I am a debtor both to Greeks and to barbarians, both to wise and unwise. So, as much as is in me, I am ready to preach the gospel to you who are in Rome also"* (vv.14, 15). A missionary heart burdened with a missionary message will be God's answer to a lost world under the wrath of God.

Paul has set forth his person and his message; he is *"not ashamed of the gospel of Christ"* (v.16). That understatement is more than supported by his missionary calling. What a challenge for us who claim to be saints and followers of the Crucified!

Chapter 2

THE GOSPEL IN ITS VERY ESSENCE

Romans 1:16, 17

Paul began his masterful epistle with a straightforward presentation of himself--a slave, an apostle, one separated to the gospel of Christ. But he turns immediately to the message, a Christ-centered message that embraces the Old Testament Scriptures and the humanity and deity of Christ. His emphasis will be on God's righteousness, our holiness in standing and state. This is a message to be shared with all nations. We are declared saints by God and entrusted with that message of grace. In fact, we are debtors to its proclamation.

The Gospel in Its Broadest Scope--Defined in Essence
Romans 1:16, 17

Nowhere else in the inspired text is the gospel presented with such crisp clarity and in depth treatment as in these two verses. There are other summations of the gospel as in 1 Corinthians 15: 3, 4; John 3:14-18 and 1 Peter 2:21-25. But here is a theological depth to Paul's condensation that includes all the major facets of God's matchless plan of salvation. In only fifty-four words, Paul, inspired by the Holy Spirit has captured the essence of the gospel which he will expand on and apply in this missionary epistle.

Presentation of the Gospel   **Romans 1:16**

Let us examine the contents of Romans 1:16. This verse is an introduction which presents:

1) Paul's reaction, not ever ashamed of his message;

2) A description of the transforming power of the gospel, a moral dynamic which changes the sinner into a saint;

3) The breadth and depth of its application, a breadth which covers race and culture and time;

4) The manner in which it is lived out in its fullness, not through human merit and effort but by saving faith - simply trusting his message;

5) With a recognition of a divine order: first Jews, God's people and then Gentiles "not a people who became a people" (1 Peter 2: 9, 10). Divine inspiration of Scripture shines clearly throughout this epistle.

Paul begins with a personal negative: *"I am not ashamed."* In reality, the gospel was his boast, but it would be most inappropriate to begin with such a self-centered statement. The gospel infinitely transcends his response to it. By means of this strong understatement, *a litotes[1]*, he declares he has never found it wanting, whether in his pilgrimage from a proud Pharisee to being a love slave of the Messiah or in his missionary endeavors.

The gospel is rather the *power of God "dúnamis"[2]*. God's creative powers are released in the moral impact of the living Word of God. Paul experienced it on the road to Damascus in his own conversion that proved genuine to the disbelief of his

---

[1] A deliberate understatement.

[2] Dynamite.

contemporaries. In Athens he faced the world's most famous philosophers and the gospel triumphed.

In Corinth the byword frequently used: to be a **"Corinthian,"** immediately identified licentious living at its very worst. In Ephesus world famous for one of the eight wonders of the world, Diana's Temple, the gospel triumphed over the sexual sins of idolatry and spiritism. Second Corinthians would be his tribute to the gospel, the power of God unto salvation. Finally, in Rome he would defy Caesar's power and die a triumphant martyr's death.

The scope of this power extends to *"salvation"* in its broadest application: forgiveness for all past sins and a new standing in justification. Biblical Christianity is the only faith to afford full assurance of the future in the face of impending death. The understanding of the legal ground of justification becomes the guarantee of true Biblical security in Christ. But justification does not stand alone but issues in holiness of life. Paul will present the Message of the Cross which cancels the power of sin (self) in progressive sanctification and the full enjoyment of eternal life.

Paul is committed to deal at length with the "how" of Christian victory. Romans 6 becomes the point of departure for the believer who desires to know who he truly is *in Christ.* There are other passages of Scripture that address this truth from different perspectives. But it can be safely said that there is no other passage that treats as deeply, as systematically and as fully as Paul's treatment of our death to the sin principle as given in Romans 6.

All of this full salvation is available to every believer on the basis of a simple faith *"to everyone who believes."* What is established is that man cannot ever offer any merit or good works in justification--and much less in sanctification. It must be the saving faith that comes by hearing. *"So then faith comes by hearing, and hearing by the word of God"* (Romans 10:17).

This simplicity of faith boggles the mind and challenges our heart. On any other basis the gospel would be impossible, because the human heart has absolutely nothing ever to offer God that he in his righteousness could possibly accept.

Finally, God has had a divine order in his mercy: *"for the Jew first and also for the Greek."* Paul will make crystal clear that salvation in its personal essence was a reality from the days of Abel, Enoch, Abraham and David. There was divine wisdom in the Old Testament in preparing Israel for her Messiah and revealing vividly God's character and the principles of faith and obedience. Paul will deal with this truth in Romans 9-11.

The Essence of the Gospel--the Righteousness of God
Romans 1:17

Paul now comes to grips with the theology of salvation. *"For in it the* **righteousness** *of God is revealed"* [is being revealed--present progressive tense]. He introduces this all important word to be understood in its depth. The **righteousness** of God is his absolute holiness in his own person and revealed as justice in the law, accepting fully only moral perfection but exercising wrath toward anything less than moral perfection.

In Romans God's righteousness has two distinct but related meanings. While we are limited in our understanding of God, we can say with confidence that his righteousness and his love are the two undergirding attributes of God; they are never in conflict but always seen in complementary action.

His holiness accepts only the absolutely perfect Jesus. On two distinct occasions of great significance we hear *"And suddenly a voice came from heaven, saying, 'This is My beloved Son, in whom I am well pleased'"* (Matthew. 3:17; 17:5). Since man cannot begin to meet the demands of the law, he must face God's holy wrath. *"Cursed is everyone who does not continue in all things which are written in the book of the law, to do them"* (Galatians 3:10).

Therefore it follows: *"For the wrath of God is revealed* [is being revealed--the same present progressive tense] *against all ungodliness and unrighteousness of men, who suppress the truth in unrighteousness"* (Romans 1:18; 3:23). But the marvel of this saving righteousness in action is that God himself made a way to meet, in a truly righteous manner, that otherwise impossible demand. He would *"set forth his own Son to be a propitiation by His blood, through faith, to demonstrate His righteousness"* (Romans 3:25).

"For when we were still without strength, in due time Christ died for the ungodly . . . But God demonstrates His own love toward us, in that while we were still sinners, Christ died for us" (Romans 5:6, 8). His holiness found a way to satisfy his own justice expressed in the law that had said: *"The soul who sins shall die"* (Ezekiel 18:4). The vicarious death of Christ for you and me is the unveiling of God's grace and mercy without in any way impugning or prejudicing his holiness.

The gospel, then, is the unveiling of the wonder of righteousness and mercy. At the Cross *"Mercy and truth have met together; righteousness and peace have kissed each other"* (Psalm 85:10). God's law was vindicated in the death of Jesus; God is now at liberty to forgive and reinstate the believing sinner. Such is justification.

The very manner in which God justifies, forgives and reinstates the sinner who believes is now called his righteousness, his own holiness in action. Paul, then, defines salvation, that is, our new position in Christ, as the righteousness of God. God's attributes of love and holiness undergird his offer of salvation.

The Manner of Receiving the Righteousness of God

The wonder of this salvation provided once for all at the Cross must now be appropriated *"from faith to faith."* It begins with faith and proceeds to its destination on that simple basis of faith. No work, effort, right living, no service, no self-denial, no religious rite can ever be added either to obtain forgiveness or retain forgiveness. It is exclusively the work of Christ at the Cross available to the believing one in simple faith.

This is simply said and written, but it is in sharp contrast and condemnation of all of our "good works," our best intentioned efforts. As salvation initially was a simple trusting for forgiveness, our sanctification is our simple trusting that we are in his Son and so we are embracing the implications of that vital union.

The Sure Foundation of the Righteousness of God

To add to the surety of this offer of righteousness/holiness is the objective truth stated four times in the Word. *"As it is written: The just shall live by faith"* (Habakkuk 2:4; Romans 1:17; Galatians 3:11; Hebrews 10:38). This salvation is not rooted in our experience, however liberating it may be. It is rooted in God's Word, in God's initiative in His Son and in our simple believing and obeying being aided by the Holy Spirit.

This eliminates forever all human boasting and fills our hearts with gratitude and humility. God has graciously ruled out human pride in any form. He reserves to himself the *"glory that he will not give to another"* (Isaiah 42:8).

Some Powerful Deductions from Paul's Briefest Statement Romans 1:16, 17

1. All the conjugated verbs are in the present tense, except the last one which is the result of God's present work of grace - justification. We have so often defined salvation as a past experience when in fact God is saving us now - sanctification (Roman 5:12-8:39).
2. Our sin is definitely implied **but not stated in these verses**, but the emphasis clearly falls on God's divine initiative; hence he will be satisfied with nothing less than that righteousness be worked out in us sanctification. He can only accept the work of Christ in us and in our behalf.
3. The emphasis falls on God's initiative and only on our response to him in faith.
4. God's salvation is an objective work of grace grounded in the transforming power of his Word.
5. All of God's benefits are ours on the basis of simple faith grounded in his gracious character.

Chapter 3

SIN AND THE MAGNITUDE OF HIS WRATH

Romans 1:18-23

In the briefest compass Paul has introduced himself: a missionary en route to Spain but an authenticated Apostle to the Gentiles. His message is Christ-centered, rooted in the deity and humanity of Jesus, the Messiah, who was forever vindicated by the Spirit of Holiness that raised him from the dead. Paul's single message is the Gospel, God's ultimate Good News to all.

After such an introduction, in two concise verses, Romans 1:16, 17, Paul defines, defends and declares the wonders of that message: the transforming power of God unto salvation, from faith to faith, to all who believe. The gospel is rooted deeply in God's righteousness that must be satisfied because of man's open rebellion; his righteousness was fully satisfied in the vicarious death of Jesus.

This gospel is from eternity past to eternity future with a strong emphasis on its present application in justification and now in our sanctification. But there is a formidable barrier to be considered before any grace can transform the sinner into the saint.

God's Holy Wrath Is Being Revealed Against Sin
Romans 1:18-23

What is most striking in Paul's masterful and systematic development of God's grace revealed in Christ is that he does NOT begin with God's mercy, not his kindness, not even his infinite love for the sinner. Those truths must wait until he has presented the death of Christ as a propitiation for the sins of all.

Paul's beginning may be a wise suggestion as to how evangelism should proceed today. We so often begin with the advantages that accrue to the sinner without much reference to the cost to God of his own Son.

A specific mention of God's infinite love does not appears in the early chapters of Romans until it appears for the first time in Rom. 5:5, 8: *"Now hope does not disappoint, because the **love of God** has been poured out in our hearts by the Holy Spirit who was given to us . . . But God demonstrates **his own love** toward us, in that while we were still sinners, Christ died for us."*

There can be no <u>Biblical appreciation</u> of the marvel of God's salvation in Christ, without a corresponding sense of the enormity of man's sin. Hence Paul begins with man's sin in the sight of a holy God.

That truth is not a commonly welcomed approach to "seeker friendly" evangelism. However, the Spirit does guide as to the approach of any given sinner. Our Lord used a variety of approaches, always with success. To Nicodemus, a morally self-sufficient teacher of the law, he used a confrontational approach (John 3); to the woman at the well he made a cultural and personal request; yet she did face her sin (John

Chapter 3: Sin and the Magnitude of His Wrath

4). But sooner or later, there must be a frank understanding of sin as God sees it.

Paul's emphasis falls on God's righteousness that must be vindicated before there can be any possible happiness or forgiveness assured. This is a totally different approach from what we usually hear in the presentation of the gospel, especially in the popular "Prosperity Gospel" approach. We are so accustomed to our needs being met, for peace and self-realization; however, the terms of God's righteousness must be met before any blessing can be ours. Sin must be atoned for and then forgiveness will come.

For the next 64 verses Paul will diagnose man's sin, the insuperable barrier that only God can remove. No other Scripture portion deals in such depth and length with the malignant cancer of sin, as does Paul's from Romans 1:18-3:20.

Paul begins abruptly by declaring: *"For the wrath of God is revealed* [is being revealed--present progressive] *from heaven against all ungodliness and unrighteousness of men, who suppress the truth in unrighteousness"* (v.18). This truth stands out as the foundational truth of salvation. It is all about God himself, his righteousness and not about man's benefit.

Notice carefully that the same verb, the same tense, *"is being revealed,"* is used with reference to his righteousness as available to save and transform the sinner in the preceding verse as is used in reference to his wrath. They are coterminous.[3] God's graciousness in offering salvation runs concurrently with his wrath against sin.

We must understand that God's wrath is NOT as our wrath. Ours is capricious, arbitrary, personally grounded in our

---

[3] Having the same or coincident boundaries.

supposed hurt. God's wrath is an extension of his holiness which is moral, measured and always just. The Creator has every right to judge the creature in rebellion. And Paul begins right there.

God's Original Provision of General Revelation and Conscience   Romans 1:19, 20

God provided fully for all the basic needs of Adam and Eve. He sends the rain on the just and the unjust. God has not left himself without a witness. God surrounded man with the vastness and greatness of a divine creation that speaks of his glory and greatness. *"The heavens declare the glory of God; and the firmament shows His handiwork. Day unto day utters speech, and night unto night reveals knowledge. There is no speech nor language where their voice is not heard. Their line has gone out through all the earth, and their words to the end of the world"* (Psalm 19:1-4).

Paul himself on Mars' Hill confirms this truth. *"And He has made from one blood every nation of men to dwell on the face of the earth . . . so that they should seek the Lord, in hope that they might grope for Him and find Him, though He is not far from each one of us; for in Him we live and move and have our being, as also some of your own poets have said. 'For we are also His offspring'"* (Acts. 17: 26-28).

To visual proof God has added an internal monitor that agrees in a limited measure with God's moral standards. Conscience still is, however, a faint echo of the original role of that moral guide that God gave to our first parents. Presently, because of sin's devastating presence, human conscience is seared, defaced and more often silenced.

God's final verdict appears: *"so that they are without excuse"* (v. 20), terse but true. Here is God's answer to the question: who are lost? General revelation and conscience bear witness to his *"eternal power and Godhead,"* but they do not save the sinner. However, they leave him without excuse. And God who knows the heart is the final judge. We may not like God's analysis, but the Creator has the right to judge his creation.

Man's Steep Descent into Depravity--Six Steps Downward
Romans 1:21, 22

In spite of the voice of creation and conscience, our forefathers, Adam and Eve and the earliest generations, left a sad trail of rebellion and disobedience. God said on the sixth day, *"Then God saw everything that He had made, and indeed it was very good"* (Genesis 1:31). *"Truly, this only I have found: that God made man upright, but they have sought out many schemes"* (Ecclesiastes 7:29).

God had placed our parents in the most idyllic circumstances imaginable. He made them the viceroys of his creation. He blessed them with the knowledge of himself, only to be tested and proven by a single simple prohibition. In the face of being granted the privilege of eating of all the other trees; only one restriction was placed on them!

Man, then, began surrounded by every blessing and honor that a gracious God could bestow and with only one condition to be obeyed--not to eat of a given tree. Such would test their faith in God and their obedience. They failed the test.

There followed six tragic steps downward, not evolution but devolution. Although Satan was the tempter in the Garden of Eden, no mention is made of his involvement in Romans' treatment of the same. Take note of that fact. There could be no one else to blame.

The guilt was clearly and equally shared by Eve, the one tempted, and Adam who chose to obey his wife rather than God who had said. *"Of every tree of the garden you may freely eat; but of the tree of the knowledge of good and evil you shall not eat, for in the day that you eat of it you shall surely die* [more literally - dying you shall die]*"* (Genesis 2:16,17).

Paul states it bluntly: *"Therefore, just as through one man sin entered the world, and death through sin, and thus death spread to all men, because all sinned"* (Romans 5:12).

The Regression of Man's Sin

Paul outlines clearly the regressive steps that culminated in man's total depravity.

"They did not glorify Him as God," Logically implicit is that they glorified themselves, just as Satan did in the primeval fall in an earlier day in heaven. In glorifying themselves at God's expense, our forefathers robbed God of his glory, the ultimate sin.

Pride was first seen in the "anointed cherub" as pictured figuratively in the king of Tyre (Ezekiel 28:13-19) and in the king of Babylon, the head of gold in Daniel's vision (Isaiah 14: 12-15; Daniel 2:38). From pride flows every other sin in multiple ways.

"Nor were thankful." The sin of pride logically becomes the sin of ingratitude. A proud self-sufficient person has no need to thank anyone. The creature becomes independent of the Creator.

"but became futile in their thoughts" Man's mind is forever distorted and deceitful. The crowning feature of God's

creation had been the ability to reason and rejoice in God's wisdom.

*"and their foolish hearts were darkened" Man's heart is sealed in darkness. Impenetrable darkness renders man's condition as final and fatal.

*"professing themselves to be wise, they became fools" Man is doubly deceived. The very attributes God gave to man, making him in his own image, now renders him doubly vain.

*"and changed the glory of the incorruptible God into an image made like corruptible man - and birds and four-footed beasts and creeping things" This was the ultimate step downward. Having robbed God of his transcendent glory, the summation of his virtues, man confers God's glory on creeping things. There is even a further descent seen in the animal kingdom, from birds to creeping things.

Man prostituted God's glory and assigned it to creeping things, no lower category possible. The Fall of Man, the entrance of sin into the world, was no minor event; it was deadly and catastrophic to the nth degree.

Man is incorrigibly depraved. His hope of salvation is utterly impossible unless God initiates his own plan of salvation. God's answer, the ultimate triumph of God's love and righteousness, came together in his Son's vicarious death and resurrection.

No wonder Jeremiah sums it up tragically: *"The heart is deceitful above all things, and desperately wicked; who can know it?"* (Jeremiah 17:9). Only now can we begin to sense the greatness of a redemption that can remove the curse and return the forgiven sinner to a position of *"heir of God and joint heir with Christ"* (Roman 8:17).

Some Powerful Deductions from God's Indictment of Man
Romans 1: 18-23

1. Man's crass rebellion merits a commensurate judgment from God.
2. God's wrath measures the enormity of the creature's sin before the Creator.
3. God's original promise for the viceroyalty was turned into open defiance toward him.
4. Man's sin was no "mistake," "weakness," "infirmity"; it was blatant rejection.
5. Doubly deceived, blinded, perverted and lost, man can offer God no good thing at all.
6. If salvation is ever to come to man, it must originate in God's justice being satisfied.
7. Man's sin in essence is my sin, my rebellion, my guilt that only Christ's blood can cover.

Chapter 4

SIN AND ITS DEBASEMENT AND EXPOSÉ

Romans 1:24-32

Paul introduces God's redemptive plan by immediately facing man's root problem – sin as God sees it, not as man conceives it. In no uncertain terms man's rebellion calls for the wrath of God. God must judge *"all ungodliness and unrighteousness of men who suppress the truth in unrighteousness"* (Romans 1:18). Having stated that basic premise, Paul outlines the voice of creation and conscience with which God gifted men in his mercy.

In spite of that offer, man took defiant steps downward (Romans 1:21-23). The initial sin was to not let God be God, to rob him of his glory and in its place glorify himself. Pride became the first sin in the prototype of Lucifer's fall and with him innumerable angels. All sins, then, devolve from that basic expression of selfishness, fierce independence of God and egotism. This is the core of man's deepest problem. How can anyone parade the goodness of man before a holy God? Blindness is personified.

Paul Charts the Course of Man's Debasement in Three Cycles Romans 1:24-28.

What follows in Romans 1:24-28 is the clearest ratification of man's sin by God. His sin is not a shortcoming, not a mere character flaw, not a slight misjudgment; sin is open, blatant rebellion that will destroy man and call down God's just wrath. That original prohibition: *"but of the tree of knowledge of good and evil you shall not eat, for in the day that you eat of it you shall surely die* [dying you will die]*"* (Genesis 2:17) will resonate through all time until eternity.

Hell became a necessity from that moment on. There could be no turning back; no human remedial action could now be taken. But God himself would find a way to triumph ultimately over man's sin and restore the forgiven sinner to a yet higher state. That transformation is the wonder, the marvel of God's love. That will become the stuff of redemption that Paul will introduce, once sin is seen as it really is in God's sight.

Cycle Number One Romans 1:24, 25

To survey these three cycles will begin to plumb the depths of sin. In our world of Postmodernism and now with its being fully expressed more openly in our culture, sin no longer is sin; it is a mistake, a mere flaw, a non-entity, if even considered at all. It is bigotry and intolerance to speak of sin as sin. The very word is taboo. To speak of God as a righteous judge infers some accountability to him and modern man recoils at that and rejects it out of hand.

But truth remains truth and error remains error. Our philosophizing will not change God's reality. Moral absolutes remain supported by God's moral government. We can do no better than quote his inspired Word: *"Therefore God also gave them up to uncleanness, in the lusts of their hearts, to dishonor their bodies among themselves, who exchanged the truth of God for the lie, and worshiped and served the creature rather than the creator, who is blessed forever. Amen"* (vv.24-25).

Paul speaks explicitly and names the sins of homosexuality and lesbianism. In fact, there is a sense of shame in even reading the graphic description of Paul as he writes from Corinth, the center of licentiousness. In spite of the philosophical advances of the Golden Age of Greek philosophers, such as Socrates, Plato and Aristotle, homosexuality abounded and was accepted as it is increasingly happening in our world today.

How some organized Protestant religions can publicly endorse practicing homosexuals to active religious leadership is proof positive to what depth of sin they have fallen! Apostasy has arrived. To the very Corinthians, infamous for their immorality, Paul wrote: *"Such were some of you. But you were washed, but you were sanctified, but you were justified in the name of the Lord Jesus Christ and by the Spirit of our God"* (1 Corinthians 6:11). In another context he warned the same Corinthians: *"And what accord has Christ with Belial? Or what part has a believer with an unbeliever? And what agreement has the temple of God with idols?"* (2 Corinthians 6:15, 16).

In virtually all the Biblical catalogues of sin, God highlights first of all any type of immorality and perversion (Mark 7:21-23; Galatians 5:19-21; Ephesians 2:1-3; Titus 3:3, 4). Such sins are the breeding ground of unclean spirits, demonic activity that leads to addiction and moral slavery.

If there is any sin that God must judge, it is the sin of evil desire, the sin closest to each of us. Whether it be the "refined" sin of covetousness (Paul's sin as a believer-- Romans 7:7) or the most gross sin of sexual addiction, there can be no forgiveness without repentance and contrition. *"Marriage is honorable among all, and the bed undefiled; but fornicators and adulterers God will judge. Let your conduct be without covetousness ..."* (Hebrews 13: 4, 5). In this first cycle God emphasizes the dishonoring of the body. Paul will develop this more fully in the next cycle.

Cycle Number Two   Romans 1:26, 27

What was referred to in the first cycle is now expanded, an explicit condemnation of homosexuality and lesbianism. This does not sit well with what is now "politically correct," but it is God's Word. *"For this reason God gave them up to vile passions. For even their women exchanged the natural use for what is against nature. Likewise also the men, leaving the natural use of the woman, burned in their lust for one another, men with men committing what is shameful, and receiving in themselves the penalty of their error which was due."* This condemnation is so explicit that no comment is needed.

Cycle Number Three   Romans 1:28

The third cycle repeats for the third time that God himself judicially ratified the free choice of man who would go his own way. *"And even as they did not like to retain God in their knowledge, God gave them over to a debased mind, to do those things which are not fitting"* (v.28). Man made his free choice of independence; God responds by ratifying it, letting sin reap its own harvest, its own punishment. How solemn to think that God three times *"gave them up"* to the consequences of their own sins! How can God be blamed for man's free choice!

God's Devastating Exposé   Romans 1:29-32

Read with shame the twenty two sins mentioned--a list by no means complete. Again the grouping of sins is so significant; as usual it begins with sexual impurities, acts of violence, attitudes, relationships Godward and manward. But the *"tiro de gracia"* [the fatal shot] is: *"Who, knowing the righteous judgment of God that those who practice such things are worthy of death, not only do the same but also approve of those who practice them"* (1:32). There can be no greater sin than such blatant defiance of God.

Puny man raises his fist in the face of God and would defy any judgment. But sin brings its own consequences, AIDS initially being one of them, but the tragedy is that now the innocent suffer with the guilty. *"Do not be deceived, God is not mocked; for whatever a man sows, that he will also reap. For he who sows to his flesh will of the flesh reap corruption, but he who sows to the Spirit will of the Spirit reap everlasting life"* (Galatians 6:7, 8).

Such sweeping statements of man's depravity can only underscore the hopelessness of man's ever saving himself. But more condemnation is yet to come in Romans 2:1-3:20. Paul is making his case for nothing less than the sovereign intervention of God in Christ, if there is ever to be any hope of salvation.

Paul is laying the groundwork for God's just condemnation of man's insatiable pride and self-righteousness. He begins with the wrath of God being revealed -- a timeless exhibition still in place today. The picture will become darker before it gets brighter. While Paul says little about repentance in Romans, his exposé of sin is such that to call for repentance is a given and needless. Judgment of sin must precede the exhibition of God's mercy and grace. But a brighter day is to dawn.

Some Powerful Deductions on Sin's Retrogression Romans 1:23-32

1. Sin like a cancer metastasizes or spreads until its deadly influence kills.
2. Man's condition is absolutely hopeless; such rebellion cannot produce any good that God can recognize. To break one law is to break them all (James 2:10).
3. God reveals his wrath against all moral lapses regardless of how the world may see them or justify them. For Christian workers this is a solemn warning. Culture provides no excuse.
4. Sin springs from the thought life and reproduces itself in acts and attitudes.
5. The prevalent sin of pornography can in no way be justified before God.
6. God the Judge is at liberty to ratify sinful choices once taken.
7. Paul's condemnation of immorality was open and evident in his day as the sin that remains in ours.

Chapter 5

SIN IN ITS MOST SUBTLE FORM--SELF RIGHTEOUSNESS

Romans 2:1- 29

In Paul's first exposé of man's critical problem (Romans 1:18-32), he faced directly the most blatant forms of sin--immorality in all its perversions: fornication, adultery, homosexuality, murder along with covetousness, envy, avarice, pride. His final condemnation is that double guilt of practicing these sins and also approving and justifying them in others (v.32). Paul wrote this exposé from Corinth, noted precisely for such sins. Against such sins God's holy wrath is being revealed (v.18).

Paul introduces dialogue as a way to interact with his reader; he uses this literary form to sharpen his argument and anticipate the response of his protagonist. It may be that his interlocutor appears to agree with Paul's stern denunciation of the gross sins of the Gentiles, but from his assured position of self-righteousness.

The religious Jew indeed viewed the Gentile, particularly the Samaritan, as basically inferior to his own righteousness before God. Paul must now denounce with a still greater fury this veiled form of sin. Without mentioning the Jew by name, he dissects the human heart, seen earlier in the Gentile but now anticipating the Jew's prevailing sin.

"*Therefore you are inexcusable, O man, whoever you are who judge, for in whatever you judge another you condemn yourself; for you who judge practice the same things*" (Roman 2:1). Then addressing such self-complacency, he follows up with a rhetorical question: "*And do you think this, O man, you who judge those practicing such things, and doing the same, that you will escape the judgment of God?*" (v.3). Paul exposes the deadly deception of the pharisaical Jew who detests the sin of the Gentile, while reveling in the far more deceitful sin of his own. Paul, as a former Pharisee, remembers well his own self-righteousness.

This contrast can be clearly seen in Jesus' denunciation of the Pharisees. With eight stern "woes", Jesus calls them: "*Serpents, brood of vipers! How can you escape the condemnation of hell?*" (Matthew 23: 33). We can measure the peril of religious self-righteousness: the tax collectors and harlots heard him gladly but the scribes and Pharisees crucified him (Matthew 21:31, 32). Jesus saw clearly the deceitfulness of self-righteousness.

Paul is more than justified in saying: "*Or do you despise the riches of His goodness, forbearance, and longsuffering, not knowing that the goodness of God leads you to repentance? But in accordance with your hardness and your impenitent heart you are treasuring up for yourself wrath in the day of wrath and revelation of the righteous judgment of God*" (vv. 4, 5).

In his denunciation of the self-righteousness of the human heart, Paul speaks of the goodness, forbearance and the longsuffering of God. Such a gracious response on God's part, even toward the sinner, is the foil that makes self-righteousness the most heinous sin that it is. We are blind to our sin of "spiritual pride," an oxymoron.

Paul in Romans speaks so clearly of the peril of this sin and the need for trust and faith that some authors have suggested that Paul did not preach repentance. How wrong can they be? He spends 64 verses (1:18-3:20) to define sin and its consequences. He hardly needs to call for repentance. But here in 2:1-5 no other conclusion can be drawn from his denunciation but that to see sin as God sees it. Repentance is a given.

Moreover, on Mars' Hill Paul, facing the proud Athenian philosophers, concluded his sermon with, *"Truly, these times of ignorance God overlooked, but now **commands all men everywhere to repent,** because He has appointed a day on which He will judge the world in righteousness by the Man whom He has ordained. He has given assurance of this to all by raising Him from the dead"* (Acts 17:30, 31).

Five Criteria by which God judges the sinner   Romans 2:1-16

In Paul's argument of God's righteous wrath against sin, he logically set forth the basis on which the Judge unleashes his wrath. It does not matter at all if the sinner be a Gentile or a Jew.

The first criterion is that God will judge the sinner according to truth. *"But we know that the judgment of God is according to truth against those who practice such things"* (v. 2). God is truth and truth will override any pretext or cultural issue.

The second criterion is that the judge is not capricious or arbitrary. Paul describes the judge as rich in *goodness, forbearance and longsuffering* (v.4); his goodness should lead to a corresponding repentance on man's part. The quality of the Judge's character denies out of hand any personal vendetta.

The third criterion is stated crisply: *"who will render to each one according to his deeds"* (v. 6). Who can call this an injustice? Man has exercised in rebellion his divinely given prerogative and deserves to receive its inevitable consequence.

The fourth criterion is that the Judge himself is the author of eternal life (v.7). His whole creation was grounded in the possible gift of eternal life. Ezekiel proclaimed: *"Say to them: 'As I live, says the Lord GOD, I have no pleasure in the death of the wicked, but that the wicked turn from his way and live'"* (33:11).

The fifth criterion is stated plainly: *"for there is no partiality with God"* (v.11). In reality God need not vindicate himself as the Creator; he is the giver of every perfect gift. Paul's criteria cannot be questioned.

The Pressing Question-The Destiny of the Lost Who Have Never Heard   Romans 2:12-16

Who has not faced the troublesome question: For those who may never have had the opportunity to hear the gospel, what is their destiny? Paul faces this relevant issue in our day when so many are saying: "many roads, many religions lead to God." This question is at the heart of all missionary endeavor. God is under no obligation to account to us for his actions. But Paul addresses the question squarely.

Abraham when interceding before God over the fate of Sodom and Gomorrah reasoned with God, *"Far be it from You to do such a thing as this, to slay the righteous with the wicked, so that the righteous should be as the wicked; far be it from*

*You! **Shall not the Judge of all the earth do right?**"* (Genesis 18:25).

Abraham's point was that there is a basic distinction between the righteous, as in this case, Lot and his family, and the wicked of those cities. In his dialoging with God, Abraham went from fifty to ten asking for mercy. God responded with fire and brimstone on the wicked, but Lot and his family were saved because they fell in that last category of ten as having been justified (2 Peter 2:7). Powerful praying!

Paul now divides mankind into two groups: the Jew who had received the law and the Gentile who never did receive the truth of God. His response is clear: *"For as many as have sinned without law* [no article] *will **also perish without law**, and as many as have sinned in* [under] *the law will be judged by the law"* (v.12). Notice carefully with regard to the Gentiles, they sinned without the principle of law (no article), only an implicit reference to the innate knowledge of truth, not a direct reference to the Law given to Moses. The Jews who sinned under law will be judged, not saved, but rather the Judge who knows the heart will decide their destiny

The issue is clear, then, that those who sin without ever hearing the gospel will perish. They have sinned and come short of the glory of God; there is no "limbo," no "purgatory," no intermediate state for a second chance.

They have sinned against the measure of light that God has given to them in creation and in conscience (Romans 1:19, 20). But Paul does expand on this truth: " . . . *for when Gentiles, who do not have the law, by nature do the things contained in the law, these, although not having the law, are a law to themselves, who show the work of the law written in their hearts, their conscience also bearing witness, and* between themselves, their thought *accusing or else excusing them* - [not saving them] *in the day when God will judge the secrets of men by Jesus Christ, according to my gospel"* (2:14-16).

In essence, the pagan who has never heard the gospel but daily responds to his measure of light or sins against the light of nature and conscience, his conscience approving or rejecting the conduct is now being considered. He will not be saved, but he will be judged by God with respect to the light he has had. Guilt remains; eternal salvation is excluded. But the inference is that there will be the mitigation of the judgment that is meted out. God has chosen to not reveal to us how he will judge. But the final issue is clear. *They will also perish without law* (v.16). But it will be according to Paul's gospel, Christ as the only savior.

Jesus himself addressed the issue: *"And you, Capernaum, who are exalted to heaven, will be brought down to Hades; for if the mighty works which were done in you had been done in Sodom, it would have remained until this day. But I say to you, that it shall be more tolerable for the land of Sodom in the day of judgment than for you"* (Matthew 11:23-24).

Paul concludes the discussion by saying that all will be judged *"by my gospel."* So sure is Paul that he speaks the mind of God; salvation will only be through the personal knowledge of Jesus Christ. These truths should be powerful motivation for reaching those who have never ever heard the gospel, powerful motivation for missions in our day.

Paul Faces the Deadly Sin of the Jews   Romans 2:17-29

Without mincing words Paul directs himself to the Jew by name: *"Indeed you are called a Jew, and rest on the law, and* make your boast in God . . . ." With some twelve apt descriptions of their privileges that God in grace had given them, he demolishes their self-righteousness with five rhetorical questions: *"You, therefore, who teach another, do you not teach yourself? You who preach that man should not steal, do you steal? You who say, Do not commit adultery, do you commit adultery? You who abhor idols, do you rob temples? You who make your boast in the law, do you dishonor God through breaking the law?"* (vv.17-24). The climax comes with the statement that levels their pride: *"For the name of God is blasphemed among the Gentiles because of you, as it is written"* (see Ezekiel 36:22). But Paul has one last devastating argument for Jewish pride and self-righteousness. The Jew considered his rite of circumcision to be his passport to heaven. It set him apart from all others as better and a member of God's special people. This religious rite given to Abraham was the last card that the self-righteous Jew could play and did play.

However, the Jew was blind to the fact that the rite was given as positive proof of Abraham's faith having waited twenty five years for God's miraculous gift of a son, thus guaranteeing the ultimate Messiah (Genesis 17).

But now Paul does the unthinkable, he "uncircumcises" the circumcised Jew by stating: *"For he is not a Jew who is one outwardly, nor is that circumcision which is outward in the flesh; but he is a Jew who is one inwardly, and circumcision is that of the heart, in the Spirit and not in the letter; whose praise is not from men but from God"* (vv. 28, 29).

Whether it be the unrighteousness of the Gentile (1:18-32) or self-righteousness of the Jew (2:1-29), God cannot tolerate either. In fact, the latter is much more deadly than the former in terms of facing it and breaking with it.

A Much Broader Application for the Believer

It would be easy to sit back and blame the Jew for self-righteousness, but the sin of "spiritual" pride was the original sin of Lucifer, that angelic creature who with free will contemplated his own God given beauty, claiming that beauty as if it were his very own. This lie gave rise to that first sin (Isaiah 14:11-15; Ezekiel 28: 12-19). Pride in its essence is egotism, selfishness, rebellion and independence of God. From that root springs every sin.

Self-righteousness blinds the heart and makes for the most dangerous of sins, both in the unsaved moral person as well the best trained Christian worker. In fact, more often than not, self-righteousness as a sin is much nearer to us in our walk with God than the sins of adultery and covetousness. **Its danger is its subtlety; its façade of holiness covers the worst sin.** Those were the areas of my own life that God had to deal with openly and harshly. Possibly the greater the giftedness, the more extensive the academic achievement, the profession of spirituality and apparent success in ministry, the greater is the danger of hypocrisy No one is immune from this besetting sin. Self-righteousness also can issue in new forms of legalism by which we judge others. May God help us!

Powerful Deductions from God's Denunciation of Self-Righteousness

1. The human heart apart from the grace of God is capable of any sin imaginable.

2. The grosser sins are calibrated as bad, the lesser sins as more tolerable.
3. The worst of sins are those that deceive us and create the illusion of piety.
4. The Gentile was condemned in Romans 1; the Jew and the human heart stand more condemned in Romans 2.
5. God-given gifts and prestige heighten greatly the temptation toward hypocrisy.
6. Only the Holy Spirit can convince the unbeliever and the **believer** of this sin.
7. In Christian work, the sin of self-righteousness is very prevalent and seldom faced for what is really is. Ministerial jealousy and envy are rooted as the very core of self-righteousness.
8. God judged the sin of Ananias and Sapphira because of their desire for a spiritual reputation equal to that of Barnabas and his wholehearted obedience (Acts 4:32-5:11). Their sin constituted a lie to the Holy Spirit and stood in the way of revival.
9. My most urgent prayer should be: Lord, deliver me from my own self-righteousness and give me only **the Righteousness of Christ,**
10. Paul's greatest desire at the end of a life time of successful ministry was: *"But indeed I also count all things loss for the excellence of the knowledge of Christ Jesus my Lord, for whom I have suffered the loss of all things, and count them as rubbish, that I may gain Christ and be found in Him **not having my own righteousness** which is from the law, but that which is through faith in Christ , the righteousness*

which is from God by faith, that I may know Him and the power of His resurrection, and the fellowship of His sufferings, being conformed to His death" (Philippians 3:8-10).

Chapter 6

GOD'S FINAL EXPOSÉ OF THE SIN NATURE

Romans 3:1-20

Paul devotes some sixty-four verses to his denunciation of the sin principle (Romans 1:18-3:20). This exposé of our sin nature is the most in-depth treatment in all of Scripture. Our informed appreciation of our *"so great salvation"* (Hebrews 2:3) is reflected in our conviction of the loathsomeness of sin. Nothing less than the death of God's own Son could remove that insuperable barrier between God and man; the magnitude of sin as a principle must be granted.

Paul begins with the wrath of God against all ungodliness (Romans 1:18); he proceeds to speak of God's General Revelation (v.19) and the entrance of sin with its six downward steps (vv. 21-23) until God three times ratifies man's rebellion (vv.24-28). Paul then lists 22 sins men practice and justify.

If that exposé appears to apply only to the Gentile, he devotes Romans 2 to the human heart in general and to the Jew in particular. The far more subtle sins of self-righteousness will be exposed for what they are: "spiritual" pride, hypocrisy, legalism, a judgmental attitude to all others with a self-forgiving tolerance for one's own sins.

All of this amounts to a defiance of God's holiness. Paul concludes by removing the Jew's false confidence in circumcision, leaving him as destitute as any Gentile--a truly masterful exposé of my heart and yours.

Paul Responds to Two Questions that Trouble the Jew
Romans 3:1-9

Paul recognizes the force of his argument, but his opponent asks a pertinent question: *"What advantage then has the Jew, or what is the profit of circumcision?"* Paul's response is immediate and positive: *"Much in every way! Chiefly because to them were committed the oracles of God* [Old Testament]" (vv.1, 2). Indeed God did privilege the Jew by entrusting him a written record of his faithfulness and salvation.

But the principle stands: much light, much more responsibility and accountability. The indictment of the Jew is that he has not believed that record but has rather set about to establish his own righteousness at God's expense. *"Brethren, my heart's desire and prayer to God for Israel is that they may be saved . . . for they being ignorant of God's righteousness, and seeking to establish their own righteousness, have not submitted to the righteousness of God"* (Romans 10:1, 3). The Jew, then, stands doubly guilty of privilege and disobedience.

One further question remains for Paul to answer. *"What, then? Are we* [Jews] *better than they? Not at all. For we have previously charged both Jew and Greeks that they are all under sin"* (Romans 3:9). Paul leaves no escape, no pretext available to the Jew or the self-righteous in his own sight. Such a resounding indictment leaves absolutely no room for any works, neither good for merit nor bad for demerit.

Paul closes the door to any salvation by which any man or woman might ever hope to enter on their own merits or efforts. The bottom line is that the human heart is lost by virtue of its own sin, be it overt unrighteousness or assumed self-righteousness. This has devastating consequences for any view of man's good works as being acceptable to God. If we were to compare one man with another man, some might appear better. But ultimately our final standing is to be judged by God's standard of perfection. We fail abysmally.

The Scriptures Themselves Condemn the Human Heart Romans 3:10-18

There is no more damning evidence in all of Scripture than this mosaic of Scripture texts; the human heart is devoid of any goodness which God could ever accept. The theologians call this **Total Depravity.** A word of caution. Total Depravity does not mean that every individual is as totally evil as he can be; nor does it imply that man may not be capable of some human goodness as a vestige of the image of God in which he was created. Horizontally toward his fellow man there may be "virtues" of patience, kindness and human love, etc.

Total depravity is, however, God's final statement of man in his vertical relationship to a holy God. In that relationship man is destitute of merit and good works. Any salvation or true holiness can never proceed from that source.

Paul's exposé of the human heart remains true for the unbeliever and **the believer who does not allow God's grace to be his motivation.** Any hope is lost that efforts proceeding from the old self nature might be acceptable to God. Paul denies any such Christian service, even done in his name, that proceeds from the flesh could ever be honored by God.

In Romans 8, the victory chapter devoted to believers, Paul states: *"So then, those who are in the flesh cannot please God"* (Romans 8:8). Here Paul is referring to the abnormality of the condition of the believer walking after the flesh and yet appearing to serve God. At the Judgment Seat of Christ such service will be *"wood, hay and stubble."*

Can there be anything clearer? *"There is none righteous, no, not one:...They have all gone out of the way; they have together become unprofitable; there is none who does good, no, not one"* (vv. 10, 12).

Paul researches the Psalms, in particular, to condemn any goodness in man that God can accept.

Almost verbatim, Paul quotes Psalm 14:1-3: *"The fool has said in his heart, 'There is no God.' They are corrupt, They have done abominable works, There is none who does good. The LORD looks down from heaven upon the children of men, to see if there are any who understand, who seek God. They have all turned aside, they have together become corrupt; There is none who does good. No, not one."*

Paul completes the mosaic of condemnation quoting from Psalm 5:9; Psalm 10:7 and Psalm 36:1. Ten times the word "No" is repeated, no, not one. The Scripture in which the Jew boasted now delivers the final blow to seal man's doom apart from the grace of God. Paul has built a waterproof argument that man is incorrigible: no hope can ever arise from within. Only a final summation follows.

God's Final Judicial Judgment on Jew and Gentile
Romans 3:19-20

We often say: "This is the bottom line, the last word." Paul sums it up by saying that God's law demands nothing less than absolute perfection; thus excluding all and any human merit. From a heart of pride, rebellion and disobedience, can any good thing come forth?

Remember what is at stake; Goodness must be good by God's absolute standard, not man's relative standard. Paul is not judging all human endeavor on the horizontal plane but rather on man's final standing before an infinitely holy God. *"Now we know that whatever the law says, it says to those who are under the law* [Jews] *that every mouth* [Gentiles] *may be stopped, and all the world may become guilty before God"* (v.19).

The final statement seals the indictment. *"Therefore by the deeds of the law no flesh will be justified in His sight, for by the law is the knowledge of sin"* (v.20). Nothing could be plainer. The legal arraignment of all flesh stands hopelessly condemned in his presence with whom we have to do. Every possibility has been exhausted, whether by "saints," philosophers, the religiously "upright" or the most bankrupt sinner. Neither merit nor demerit has prevailed.

This does deny the human heart of its ever realizing salvation on its own merits in the presence of a holy God. But here is precisely where the grace and love of God appear. With an about face Paul asserts: *"But now the righteousness of God apart from the law is revealed..."* (v. 21). We leave the darkness of sin (Romans 1:18-3:20) to enter the glorious light of the Gospel (3: 21-31).

Some Powerful Deductions from God's Exposé of Sin

All have sinned [present perfect tense] and fall short [present tense] of the glory of God.

1. A holy God cannot accept anything less than his law's demands--absolute perfection and, as such, man has fatally failed.
2. God's only Son did, however, achieve God's full acceptance: *"This is my beloved son, in whom I am well pleased"* (Matthew 3:17). A way has now been opened for the lost sinner.
3. By extension the human heart, unaided by the grace of God, cannot serve God acceptably. This is God's final verdict for the sinner and the saint who would serve in the energy of the flesh for self-glory or self-realization.

Chapter 7

THE MARVEL OF THE GRACE OF GOD: A NEW RIGHTEOUSNESS

Romans 3:21-24

From Romans 1:18 through 3:20 the General Revelation of God in creation and conscience, and now the Mosaic law, have all thundered against the sins of mankind. With sixty four unrelenting continuous verses (1:18-3:20), Paul under the inspiration of the Holy Spirit will allow absolutely no merit or inherent worth in man's best intentioned efforts.

The logical consequence can only be that mankind, be he or she Jewish or Gentile, is and will be totally bereft of any hope of salvation based on his own works. Mankind has come to the end of the line.

But with the matchless marvel of God's grace in view, Paul now does a hundred and eighty degree turn about and introduces with majestic assurance that salvation is at hand by the expressed initiative of God, the holy Judge.

In one sense from the most unexpected source imaginable, from the holy Judge himself, comes the issuance of the valid offer of righteousness; the offer is nothing less than the very righteousness of his own Son.

God the Father had affirmed his Son's righteousness at his baptism: *"This is My beloved Son, in whom I am well pleased"* (Matthew 3:17) and at the transfiguration (Luke 9:35). He verified it once and for all by the resurrection of our Substitute and Sin Bearer: *"And declared to be the Son of God with power, according to the Spirit of holiness, by the resurrection from the dead"* (Romans 1:4).

Since man has no righteousness of his own, salvation, if there is to be any salvation at all, must be God's righteousness reckoned to the believing sinner. That is precisely the marvel of his matchless grace. Paul will now expound on how God does it.

The Righteous Judge Announces His Gracious Salvation
Romans 3:21-23

All theologians agree that Romans 3:21-26 is the classic Biblical definition of salvation. Nothing is more concise, profound and inclusive that these few verses. They can never be fully plumbed for depth of meaning. Paul begins with the adversative conjunction: **"but now"**--two simple words, an emphatic logical transition, that reverse the whole thrust of the previous verses (1:18-3:20). From another source so unexpected comes the offer of God's righteousness.

Here we pause to make clear there are two expressions of different and yet related meanings to the theological term the **"righteousness of God."**

1.) His righteousness in its most explicit form was the Mosaic Law that epitomized God's holiness and righteous demands. The Mosaic Law was the transcript of the absolute righteousness of God, his primary attribute. But Paul has already established that that Law has *"stopped the mouth of every man"* (vv.19, 20). On the contrary, the knowledge of sin comes by that law. That law, then, could never save, much less sanctify, but rather it can only condemn the sinner. Where does that leave us?

2.) Now comes the gracious announcement with a **new aspect** to be introduced: *"But now the righteousness of God apart from the law is revealed, being witnessed by the Law and the Prophets, even the righteousness of God, which is though faith in Jesus Christ to all and on all who believe"* (vv.21, 22, cf., *"for in it the righteousness of God is revealed. 1:17)."* Where no hope existed, when every supposed merit of man was denied, no salvation was possible. But Paul affirms that this gracious salvation was nothing new or strange!

He says: *"But now the righteousness of God **apart from the law** is* [having been revealed - perfect passive participle] *revealed, being witnessed by the Law and the Prophets."* He is saying, in effect that the Old Testament already teaches God's unique personal plan of salvation. We must be prepared to find it in the Pentateuch and the Prophets.

No one less than Jesus himself testifies to that effect. *"You search the Scriptures, for in them you think you have eternal life; and these are they which testify of Me"* (John 5:39). And to the two on the road to Emmaus Jesus is described stating: *"And beginning at Moses and all the Prophets, He expounded to them in all the Scriptures the things concerning Himself"* (Luke 24:27).

Paul has asserted clearly that this righteousness, a new judicial position, must be found in the prophecies and covenants in the Old Testament. Paul is not introducing anything new and novel in terms of the truths of personal salvation, that is, the love of God, the grace of God and faith in the promised Messiah.

The "Protevangelium" announced God's Intervention Genesis 3:15.

The most outstanding and earliest prophecy is Genesis 3.15. The early fathers called it the "Protevangelium,"[4] not only the very first prophecy but the prototype, the pattern of future prophecies to come, the first "Gospel" announcement. Immediately after Adam and Eve had sinned, God asked Adam the simple question: *"Where are you?"* Adam responded: *"I hid because I was naked"* (vv.9, 10) and there followed a second question in which he blamed God: *"The woman you gave to be with me..."* Eve in a similar vein blamed the serpent.

Then to the serpent, God categorically announced his irrevocable curse. To our surprise, he announced to Satan in the presence of Adam and Eve the very strategy he would employ to defeat Satan and rescue and save the guilty pair. No military general announces his plan of action to the enemy. But our sovereign God was on the move immediately and no one could prevent his triumph.

Five Dramatic Pronouncements:

1) *"I will put enmity"*--The sovereign initiative of God to establish once and for all his absolute wrath on Satan and sin.

2) *"I will put enmity between you and the woman"*--The very agent of sin, a woman, would in grace become God's choice to accomplish his purpose. *"Behold the*

---

[4]George W. Peters, *A Biblical Theology of Missions*, (Chicago: Moody Press) 1972, pp. 85, 86. I am indebted to my former professor for introducing me to this significant prophecy in my missiological doctoral studies.

Chapter 7: The marvel of the grace of God -- a new righteousness virgin shall conceive and bear a Son, and shall call His name Emmanuel" (Isaiah 7:14), the clear promise of a Messiah.

3) *"And between your seed and her Seed"*--Two different seeds of mankind were now committed to spiritual warfare: Abel, Enoch, Abraham, Moses, David versus Cain, Lamech, the antediluvians and those of the Tower of Babel down to this present day.

4) *"He will bruise your head"*--The Messiah will deal a death blow to the head, fatal and final. Christ did this once for all at the Cross: *"Now is the judgment of this world; now the ruler of this world will be cast out"* (John 12: 31).

5) *"and you will bruise His heel"*--It would be through suffering, the Cross, that God's wrath on his own Son would be a temporary but real blow, but his resurrection would be proof positive of God's acceptance of his Son's vicarious death.

In retrospect, we have the benefit of history to see clearly what God in his sovereignty had already ordained to be done, the gracious rescue of his own.

Other Witnesses to God's Intervention in the Old Testament

God's Abrahamic Covenant promised him a son. In the midst of that long wait of 25 years, God renewed that covenant some three times. Scripture says: *"And he believed in the LORD, and He accounted it to him for righteous"* (Genesis 15:6). Paul quotes the text verbatim in Romans 4:3 as proof of the New Testament righteousness.

Later God would make the inconceivable demand that Abraham's only son, the heir of the promise, must be sacrificed. Abraham proceeded in faith to the very moment of slaying Isaac, but God provided a ram caught in a thicket, a substitute (Genesis 22). What we witness in Abraham is a virtual Old Testament Calvary.

However, in the New Testament Calvary there was no substitute found. *"In due time, Christ died for the ungodly"* (Romans 5:8). *"He who did not spare His own Son, but delivered Him up for us all, how shall He not with Him also freely give us all things?"* (Romans 8:32). Little wonder Christ said: *"Your father Abraham rejoiced to see My day, and he saw it and was glad"* (John 8:56).

The preparations for the Passover were a dramatization of Calvary. The blood of the Pascal lamb was applied to the door posts and lintel granting protection from the Angel of Death; the feasting in the home on the flesh of the lamb, the eating of bitter herbs and the feet shod with readiness to leave, all speak loudly of our standing as protected by his blood from divine wrath and **in participating in the flesh of the Pascal lamb, thus sharing in the very risen life of Christ** (Exodus 12; John 6:35-58). This very important latter aspect has long been overlooked in favor of the first aspect of the covering of the blood.

The Annual Day of Atonement marked the removal of the sins of ignorance, a limited yearly symbolical covering (Leviticus 16). Only the High Priest once a year could enter, once for himself and a second time for the people. This high Sabbath reminded them of the insufficiency of the Levitical system. It provided a shadow of what was to come but not the substance. *"But in those sacrifices, there is a reminder of sins every year. For it is not possible that the blood of bulls and goats could take away sins"* (Hebrews 10:3, 4).

Finally, the capstone of all prophecies is the Isaiah prediction, not of a lamb but rather the Messiah himself. No clearer description, even in the New Testament, could ever be made than Isaiah's masterpiece. *"Yet it pleased the LORD to bruise Him; He has put him to grief. When You make His soul an offering for sin, He shall see His seed, He shall prolong His days, And the pleasure of the LORD will prosper in His hand. He shall see the travail of His soul, and be satisfied. By His knowledge My righteous Servant shall justify many"* (Isaiah 53: 10, 11).

Paul is not adding anything new to God's plan of **personal salvation;** he is rediscovering the earliest promises of the Messiah who would *"bruise the serpent's head."*

The Righteousness of God Introduces a New <u>Position</u> of Acceptance and Favor

Note carefully that Paul says*: "the righteousness of God...is revealed* [is being revealed]*."* This is the present perfect tense, passive voice, that is, his righteousness stands ever available on his conditions. This righteousness has been as available to Old Testament saints as readily as to Paul's readers, but always on God's terms of faith. The precise content and historical knowledge may not have been identical, that is, before the Cross and after the Cross, but the essential element is faith in God's promise of grace which is common to both ages.

If the reality of personal saving faith in the Old Testament is ever questioned, Hebrews eleven is the standing monument to the genuine faith of the Old Testament saints. They believed in the clarity of divine prophecies, even in the face of far less historical data. *"These all died in faith, not having received the promises, but having seen them afar off were assured of them, embraced them, and confessed that they were strangers and pilgrims on the earth"* (Hebrews 11:13).

While differences do exist between God's plan for Israel and the church, between the Old and New Testament, there has always been only one way of personal salvation--not an inferior salvation versus a superior salvation. What was implicit in the Old Testament before the Cross becomes explicit with the added new reality of the Church invisible, the Body of Christ.

Paul makes it crystal clear that this righteousness is through faith in Christ without distinction of race, economic status or gender. It is *"even the righteousness of God, which is through faith in Jesus Christ to all and on all who believe. For there is no difference; for all have sinned and fall short of the glory of God"* (vv. 22, 23). One can feel the breadth and depth of this sweeping statement. No mention is made here of the doctrine of election--a Biblical doctrine as explained and set forth in Romans 8:28-30, where it is rightly balanced with God's gracious sovereignty.

Paul returns to the sweeping indictment of Romans 1:18-3:20. Sin cannot be minimized or discounted. There is absolutely no advantage given to any. All are destitute of any possible merit or advantage. Today there is abroad a minimizing of the reality of man's perversity and condemnation. Self helps, feeling good about one's self, avoiding the offence of the Cross, not wanting to offend the sinner, all such false gospels fail to deal deeply with man's total depravity and abject need for God's righteousness offered in Christ to the sinner who repents and believes.

Paul sums up the genuine offer of God to mankind from Genesis onward. *"Being **justified freely** by His grace thorough the redemption that is in Christ Jesus"* (v. 24). With a double emphasis on the gracious redemption, Paul assigns to God alone the genuine offer of forgiveness. Salvation is not only the forgiveness of sins but a **new standing, a legal standing, secure, unalterable** and **based exclusively on the merits of Christ's death and resurrection.** Salvation can have no more sure *"foundation than that which is laid, which is Jesus Christ"* (1 Corinthians 3:11).

Deductions for Our Gracious Salvation through Christ

1. When all hope of salvation was forever lost to mankind, God intervenes in grace and announces the salvation that meets his ultimate standards for righteousness.
2. That standard of righteousness is nothing less than God's own righteousness found in the God-man who took our place in death to sin and now is alive to God (Romans 6:10).
3. To that standard nothing can be added nor taken from it. It is final, absolute, secure.
4. Paul says and will say again and again that righteousness is ours by believing from the heart, totally apart from merit or works.
5. Everyone sinned [past tense] and fall short or are destitute [present state] of the glory of God (3:23); hence if there is to be any salvation at all, it must be his giving of righteousness to unworthy believers, now *"being freely justified by His grace."*

6. Salvation begins and ends with God's grace extended in Christ to whoever believes.

CHAPTER 8

THE MARVEL OF THE GRACE OF GOD – A NEW STANDING IN HIM

Romans 3: 25-31

Paul has set forth in Romans 3:21-24 the basic facts of God's matchless marvel of grace: there is a righteousness that meets the Judge's absolute standard, nothing less than the righteousness of his own Son (3:21). This salvation was announced to God's original creation, witnessed to by the Mosaic law that condemned man's best (v.21); a righteousness imputed to all sinners without exception on the sole condition of faith (vv.22,23); such a righteousness freely given is grounded in the redemption or purchase price ["*kofer*"] of his Son (v.24). There is no fine print that negates this offer of grace.

We so often repeat: Christ died for our sins. We are saved through his death. Christ died for me. These are all basic truths of which we can never be ashamed (Romans 1:16, 17). But seldom do we ask ourselves on what basis does God forgive our sins? How does he do it ethically? These are the precise questions that Paul will answer and address in this classic passage.

On What Ethical Basis Does God Forgive our Sins?

We must remember that God is a holy Judge. His primary attribute that defines him is his holiness, holy wrath toward sin and therefore indirectly toward the sinner. We often hear: God hates sin but loves the sinner. True, but these two facts are combined in one person.

Paul faces this paradox head on. What God has done in salvation is now called his *"righteousness,"* the second meaning of the term righteousness; the first was his attribute, the second being now the new *position* granted to the sinner who believes. God's salvation is called the righteousness of God (Romans 1:17), nothing more, nothing less.

The Law and the Prophets Provide the Context of Our Salvation

The Mosaic Law in governing the social life of the Israelite grants the right of a substitute to be provided in case of a rare and unequal demand. Under the early code of the law, if an ox gored to death a man or a woman, the ox would be stoned to death and the owner put to death. Such a double death would be an unequal demand. However, *"If there is imposed on him a sum of money, then he shall pay to redeem his life, whatever is imposed on him"* (Exodus 21: 29, 30). The payment to be valid must be assigned or approved by a judge. No such arrangement was possible for a murderer (Numbers 35:31). In a given case, there was, then, an ethical price paid to redeem the life at stake

In addition, the Law of Moses had said: *"Keep yourself far from a false matter; do not kill the innocent and righteous.* ***For I will not justify the wicked"*** (Exodus 23:7). Now to provide for our salvation God would have to do precisely what he promised he could not do. However, in his sovereign wisdom there was a way ethically to do just that, without in any way prejudicing his character or compromising his law.

God found a truly just way to satisfy his own law and yet forgive the sinner in the person of his divinely appointed substitute. Only an infinite sinless being could adequately cover the sins of finite beings against an infinite God. The holy Judge let his wrath fall on his own Son, through the vicarious death of the law keeper, *"For there is one God and one Mediator between God and men, the Man Christ Jesus who gave Himself a ransom* ["kofer," ransom price paid] *for all, to be testified in due time"* (1 Timothy 2: 3-6).

In a nutshell Romans 3:25 is at the very heart of the righteousness of God available to us through faith. *"Whom God set forth to be a propitiation by His blood, through faith, to demonstrate His righteousness* [salvation], *because in His forbearance God had passed over the sins that were previously committed."* The verb "to set forth" simply means to manifest, proposed as a previous design. This is the crucial nature of the timing of his death.

This special verb could refer to the "Protevangelium" of the ancient church fathers. A new airplane is first built as a prototype; all subsequent planes are the exact mechanical duplicates of this one proven design. Hence God was building his prototype in the Old Testament preparing the way for the timely arrival of the Messiah.

Isaiah could not have expressed it more succinctly: *"All we like sheep have gone astray; We have turned everyone, to his own way: and the* **LORD has laid on Him the iniquity of us all** *. . . Yet it pleased the LORD to bruise Him; He has put Him to grief. When You make His soul an offering for sin, He shall see*

His seed, He shall prolong His days, and the pleasure of the LORD shall prosper in His hand" (Isaiah 53:6, 10).

With the echo of that Messianic prophecy we hear it now clearly in Paul's concise presentation of "how" God the Judge could and does forgive guilty sinners. *"Whom God has set forth to be a propitiation by His blood, through faith, to demonstrate His righteousness..."* (v.25).

In New Testament terms Paul said: *"But when the fullness of the time had come, God sent forth His son, born of a woman, born under the law to redeem* [buy back] *those who are were under the law, that we* [he writes to Gentiles] *might receive the adoption of sons"* (Galatians 4:4,5).

The Significance of the Day of Atonement--the Role of the Mercy Seat   (Leviticus 16)

Once again the Old Testament is crucial to our grasp of the principles of divine righteousness and God's love for the sinner. The Day of Atonement or Yom Kippur was a High Sabbath occurring once a year, on the tenth day of the seventh month--significant the dates: tenth--fullness, seventh--a divine number.

The context of the first Day of Expiation was the sin of Aaron's two sons who offered profane fire and died. The day was to highlight forever that there would be an approach to a holy God, but only with severe limitations. *"Tell Aaron your brother not to come at simply any time into the Holy Place inside the veil before the mercy seat . . . lest he die. For I will appear in the cloud above the mercy seat* (v.2).

Hebrews reveals the symbolic essence of the "how" to approach a holy God from the backdrop of the Day of Atonement: *"But into the second part the high priest went alone once a year, not without blood, which offered for himself and the people's sins committed in ignorance; the Holy Spirit indicating this, that the way into the Holiest of All was not yet made manifest while the first tabernacle was still standing. It was symbolic for the present time...imposed until the time of reformation"* (Hebrews (9:7-10).

The Hebrew verb "kipper"[5] to expiate, to cover, has several variant uses all related to Biblical usages: "kofer"--the ransom price paid to redeem; "kapporeth"--the mercy seat. In Spanish which is the language of my ministry, the words are almost identical: mercy seat--"propiciatorio" and propitiation --"propiciación," the act of covering.

Above the mercy seat God's presence was revealed in Shekinah glory; the mercy seat itself was actually the golden cover of the Ark of the Covenant which housed the two tablets of a broken law. With the blood sprinkled seven times over the mercy seat, God could not see the two tablets of a broken law. The shed blood of the lamb appeased the wrath of God; his law was satisfied, releasing him to be propitious toward the sinner. A substitute had died vicariously and the Judge has accepted the covering.

Christ as the **propitiation for our sins** is at the very heart of our salvation. **Propitiation is the gracious effect on God's justice or violated holiness by virtue of the vicarious death of his son enabling God to express his love and forgive our sin.** The Father's offering of his own Son validated him as a sin offering and freed God to be what he always was and is, a God

---

[5] F. J. Pop, *Palabras bíblicas y sus significados* (Biblical Words and Their Meanings), (Buenos Aires: Editorial Escaton), 1972, pp. 303-307. I discovered this unique book on a trip to Argentina which compares Hebrew, Greek, Aramaic words with a variety of versions of the past.

of love. There could now be no tension between his love and his righteousness.

Because Christ as our propitiation was God's original eternal design, he could pass over the full execution of the law on earlier sinners. David's sin of murder and adultery would and should have been his death by stoning. But he rejoices in God's forgiveness: *"Blessed is he whose transgression is forgiven, whose sin is **covered**. Blessed is the man to whom the LORD **does not impute** iniquity, and in whose spirit there is no guile"* (Psalm 32:1, 2). Such an apparent overlooking of the execution of the Law's 'wrath could easily have left a shadow on God's character; either God flouted his own law or was powerless to enforce it. Neither alternative was true.

David in faith looked to the coming Messiah, knowing that in God's timeless love, a fully adequate removal of sin was to be exhibited on the Cross (Rom. 3:26). All of God's timeless provisions in his Son, our Substitute, are ours as were those available to the Old Testament saints by simple faith.

God's only condition for them and for us was a heart faith and trust. The Cross forever removes a possible shadow from his having passed over our sins. He then is *"just and the justifier of one who has faith in Jesus"* (v.25).

The Judge's Final Declaration: Jew and Gentile are Justified by Faith   Romans 3:28-31

If the holy Judge is to remain holy, no possible question can be raised about his exercise of forgiveness for the guilty. God remains holy beyond all moral questions. Christ became our substitute taking our sin, being our propitiation; we have taken his righteousness. God on his own terms is both just and the justifier of the sinner who believes. True believing faith subsumes heart repentance.

Furthermore, since God the Father initiated and God the Son executed his redemptive plan, any one so forgiven and restored can never boast of his or her righteousness. Both Jew and Gentile all condemned under the law are offered the wonder of **God's Grand Design** and stand before him in the fully imputed righteousness of God himself (vv. 27-30). God in the last analysis is totally just. No advantage is given to Jew or Gentile, both stand equally condemned under the law (v.20) but equally justified by faith apart from the deeds of the law.

Powerful Deductions from our Gracious Salvation through Christ.

1. God's intervention is seen in Genesis 3:15 in the first words pronounced after man's fall, words directed against the serpent by which he established his salvific design through the *"Seed of the Woman."*

2. The whole Old Testament testifies to the principle of expiation or substitution: *"Behold! The Lamb of God that takes away the sin of the world!"* (John 1:29).

3. God waited for the law to expose the heinousness of sin and timed Christ's death on the Cross at that crucial moment to unveil his gracious gift of righteousness.

4. With man totally depraved, redemption could only come from God on his terms, grace *"through faith, and that not of works lest anyone should boast"* (Ephesians 2:8.9).

5. God has cut the "Gordian knot" and found a just way to forgive and restore the repentant and believing sinner. To God be the glory!
6. Christ is *"the propitiation for our sins, and not for ours only but also for the whole world"* (1 John 2:2).

Chapter 9

JUSTIFYING FAITH IN ABRAHAM AND DAVID

Romans 4: 1-15

Paul has set forth his masterful presentation of the righteousness of God in the classic passage, Romans 3: 21-31. Salvation is a legal judgment and position by which God declares the believer righteous on the ground of faith in his Son's vicarious death. God has justified the ungodly: *"But to him who does not work, but believes on Him who justifies the ungodly, his faith is accounted for righteousness"* (Romans 4:5).

In the marvel of God's redemptive plan three means of salvation have coalesced in the classic passage. The primary means of salvation is the **grace of God**, a gracious initial dynamic flowing from God's character--*"being justified freely by his grace"* (3:24).

The second means of salvation is the **shedding of Jesus' blood,** as a voluntary substitute as set forth by the Judge himself as a sin offering. *"being justified freely by his grace through the redemption that is in Christ Jesus, whom God set forth to be a propitiation by his blood, through faith to demonstrate His righteousness"* (vv.24, 25). His death was an expiation, a covering for sin and thus freeing the righteous Judge in love to forgive the sinner.

The third means of salvation is *faith,* that divine/human response to the marvel of his grace and vicarious death. With no merit or ability of his own, the sinner moved by the power of the Word and the Holy Spirit reaches out an empty hand and receives the gift of righteousness. There are eight references to faith in this passage (Romans 3: 21-31).

Three Laws of Divine Expiation

There must be **satisfaction** on God's part with regard to the quality of the substitute. The Judge alone determines the substitute's viability. Therefore the Old Testament animal sacrifices could never remove man's sin. The Old Testament sacrifice could only cover sin ceremonially and temporarily. It would only point the way to God's substitute (Isaiah 53) with whom he was fully satisfied.

There must be **solidarity** between the substitute and the sinner. *"Inasmuch then as the children have partaken of flesh and blood, He Himself likewise shared in the same, that through death He might destroy him who had the power of death, that is, the devil, and release those who through fear of death were all their lifetime subject to bondage"* (Hebrews 2:14, 15).

There must be **sympathy** on the part of the substitute to give his life willingly for another. *"Therefore, when He came into the world, He said: Sacrifice and offering You did not desire, But a body you have prepared for me . . . Behold, I have come to do Your will , O God"* (Hebrews 10:5, 9).

Paul has much more to say about the role of faith and so devotes a full chapter -- Romans 4 -- to its function and its relevancy for today's believer. Because works and faith are mutually exclusive and incompatible and because the law placed such a stress on works, Paul must carefully establish the role of faith as opposed to the works of the law.

Abraham, the Example of Justifying Faith before the Law Was Given   Romans 4: 1-5

The Jewish rabbis had virtually lifted Abraham to automatic sainthood, attributing to him a sanctity beyond all others by virtue of his works. Paul selects their prime example and asks the simple question: Was Abraham justified by his works? He answers it simply: *"Not before God."*

A straightforward quotation suffices to silence such a thought: *"Abraham believed God, and it was accounted to him for righteousness"* (Genesis 15:6; Romans 4:3). It is important to address the context of Genesis 15. Abraham had just rescued Lot and was blessed by Melchizedek to whom he paid tithes (Genesis 14). After this high point of faith, Jehovah appeared to him and said: *"I am your shield, your exceedingly great reward."*

Abraham countered with a logical suggestion. Years had passed since Ur and the covenant promise of a son but he was still childless. Could a son born in his cultural household qualify? God responded: by no means, he would have a son by faith but in God's time. In that instance Abraham believed the promise and only the promise and was ***declared righteous*** "sola fide."

Can Works Play any Role in Justification?

Having established the exclusive role of faith, Paul turns to the logical incompatibility between these two principles. Works or any human participation implies a contract between two more or less equals. Before a holy God it would imply the right of man to demand of God recognition for effort, no matter how small. But it is unthinkable that any mortal man could stand in his holy presence. The sinner has absolutely nothing to offer God and so works must be ruled out of hand as out of the question.

The only other alternative is to not work but to cast oneself on God's grace. The only avenue open to such a bankrupt sinner is to believe, to trust. So Paul states it clearly: *"But to him who does not work, but believes on Him who justifies the ungodly, his faith is accounted for righteousness"* (v.5). Abraham believed God and God reckoned his faith for righteousness.

David, the Example of Justifying Faith after the Law Was Given Romans 4:6-8

David, even after his heinous sins of adultery and premeditated murder (2 Samuel 11), wrote: *"Blessed is he whose transgression is forgiven, **whose sin is covered.** Blessed is the man to whom the LORD **does not impute** iniquity"* (Psalm 32: 1, 2). Such verses do not minimize the grievous sins of David, for he repented with a full confession of his sins (Psalm 51). God, however, never did revoke David's righteous standing before Him. When God declares the ungodly righteous on the basis of his faith in Christ's blood, the believer remains forever dressed in that righteousness that pleases God.

God never grants the believer license to sin. Inevitably and implacably the consequences of discipline and judgment will follow. Fellowship will have been broken, but it can be restored though confession and the cleansing of the blood. God in his mercy may mitigate some of the practical consequences, even as in David's case, but he will never dismiss them out of hand. No one can sin with impunity.

For the one who truly is justified in the sight of God, his standing remains forever secure. Christ's death and its imputed righteousness will stand as long as Christ's righteousness prevails before His Father. God himself has committed Himself forever: *"This is My beloved Son, in whom I am well pleased"* (Matt.3:17). That standing in His righteousness is our only assurance of heaven. No amount of service or faithfulness can ever add to that quality of righteousness.

However, not everyone who may claim to be saved may be truly justified. God Himself is the ultimate Judge and our subsequent lives should give evidence of the fruit of righteousness. The perfect balance of these truths is Paul's counsel: *"Nevertheless the solid foundation of God stands, having this seal: 'The Lord knows those who are His,' and, 'Let everyone who names the name of Christ depart from iniquity'"* (2 Timothy 2:19).

"Now Faith is the Substance...the Evidence of Things Not Seen" Hebrew 11:1

What is the essence of faith? The writer to the Hebrews may not give us a technical definition of faith, but he does describe its basic qualities. **It is substance and evidence that will manifest itself in future reality**. It lets God be God; he began the work in grace through faith and he will finish the work in grace through faith. Such a faith is grounded in the veracity of God's character which is "legal tender" for his promises.

I liken faith to an outstretched hand, open and empty and ready to receive from the gracious giver what is offered and what is urgently needed. Dr. F. J. Huegel, my mentor (1957-68), used to say: "Praise or thanksgiving is faith in full bloom." What he gives, we take and thanksgiving is our only response possible. There can be no merit in such receiving.

Abraham justified by faith without works becomes the father of the faithful. *"And if you are Christ's, then you are Abraham's seed, and heirs according to the promise"* (Galatians 3:29). Let faith with grace reign in your heart and mine!

Powerful Deductions from the Role of Faith in the Believer's Life

1. There is no more basic and concise definition of the Christian life than *"**The just shall live by faith**"* (Habakkuk 2:4; Romans 1:17; Galatians 3:11; Hebrews 10:38--four distinct textual quotes).

2. Faith and works--efforts, service rendered, faithfulness attempted, years of relative success or recognition -- are mutually exclusive in terms of merit and worth before God. God only recognizes his Son's righteousness, never the flesh's feeble attempts.

3. **Romans 4:16-25 will apply this basic faith principle to sanctification and service.** This is a truth virtually lost in our "works righteousness mentality" so common in Christian ministry today.

4. Sanctification or victory in Christ is by faith every bit as much as is justification by faith. We agree easily with the latter but fail to grasp the role of faith in the former. Anything less than the exclusivity of faith before God compromises the work of the Cross. *"If righteousness comes through the law"*--our best efforts--*"then Christ died in vain"* (Galatians 2:21).

Chapter 10

WITH ABRAHAM IN THE SCHOOL OF FAITH

Romans 4:13-25

Paul dedicates the whole of Romans 4 to the role of faith, that divine/human quality that brings God's justifying grace. When I say a **divine/**human means of grace, the order of the words is highly significant.

Paul has stated clearly: *"For I say, through the grace given to me, to everyone who is among you, not to think of himself more highly than he ought to think, but to think soberly, as **God has dealt to each one a measure of faith"** (Romans 12: 3).

Again Paul states in the classic New Testament passage of salvation: *"For by grace you have been saved through faith, and that **not of yourselves;** it is the gift of God not of works, lest anyone should boast"* (Ephesians 2:8, 9). Faith could never have its origin and its dynamic in the believer. In God's inscrutable way, the Holy Spirit produces the response of faith in the believer. *"So then faith comes through hearing and hearing by the word of God"* (Romans 10:17). *"And take the helmet of salvation and the sword of the Spirit, which is the Word of God"* (Ephesians 6:17).

But if faith is first of all the divine quality, it is bound up with the believer's response; hence that empty hand that reaches out in obedient hope and receives what God gives. With no outstretched hand, there can be no reception of what God offers in grace. Here in the juncture of faith, we stand back in awe of God's sovereign purposes. By grace through faith on the basis of the Christ's blood, God gives the fullness of his salvation. *"For I am not ashamed of the gospel of Christ, for it is the power of God to salvation to **everyone who believes**"* (Romans 1:16).

Five stages in Abram's Developing Faith   Genesis 12, 15, 17, 21, 22

To speak of faith one turns immediately to the "father of faith, Abraham." God appeared to Abram while still in Ur of the Chaldees and made a covenant promising him a land and a son. God had said: *"I will make you a great nation; I will bless you and make your name great; And you shall be a blessing... And in you all families of the earth shall be blessed"* (Genesis 12: 2, 3). Abram's immediate obedience proved his faith in God's covenant. *"By faith Abraham obeyed . . . And he went out, not knowing where he was going"* (Hebrews 11:8). The **first stage** took place when Abram was 75.

But Abram's faith was to be tested and would grow. Some years later in Genesis 15, God would intervene in the **second stage** of Abram's developing faith. *"After these things the word of the LORD came to Abram in a vision, saying: 'Do not be afraid, Abram. I am your shield, your exceedingly great reward* [El Shaddai]'" (Genesis 15: 1-7).

Abram was expecting a son as promised in the covenant and so suggested to God that his servant Eliezer's son born in his house might be the fulfillment of the promise. God said: "In no way" and showed him the stars as proof of the future nations that would call him blessed. Moses' report of this second confirmation of the Abrahamic Covenant is quoted verbatim in Romans 4: 3: *"For what does the Scripture say? 'Abraham believed God, and it was accounted to him for righteousness.'"* Here was proof positive of the personal justification of Abram anticipating New Testament personal salvation.

Twelve years had passed and still no son. Abram is 87. Sara now suggests a son by way of Hagar, her Egyptian slave. Abram's faith falters and Ishmael is born. This was not the only time that Abram's faith had faltered. Faith is often weak, but God would once again take the initiative and be true to his promise.

In Genesis 17 *"When Abram was ninety nine years old, the LORD appeared to Abram and said to him: I am Almighty God; walk before Me and be blameless."* In the **third stage** God expands the covenant promise in greater detail and introduces circumcision as the **sign of his faith**. With this sign of a cutting off of the old to add something new, God changes Abram's name to Abraham – *"father of many nations."* (17:5). Abram is now 99 and God is about to announce the miraculous birth of Isaac in Genesis 17:16.

The **fourth stage** had now come after all human hope of a biological son had disappeared. *"And the LORD visited Sarah as He had said, and the LORD did for Sarah as he had spoken"* (21:1). Isaac was born. The faith of Abraham had been rewarded and even Sarah finds her place in the gallery of faith heroes in Hebrews 11: 11: *"By faith Sarah, even Sarah, received strength to conceive seed, and she bore a son when she was past the age, because she judged Him faithful who had promised."*

The **fifth stage** was yet to come when God would ultimately test Abraham's faith in Genesis 22 to the nth degree. *"Take now your son, your only son Isaac, whom you love, and go the land of Moriah, and offer him there as a burnt offering."* We know the story of God's intervention in the last moment. Hebrews 11: 17-19 tell us that in that ultimate act of obedient faith, Abraham glimpsed the resurrection that must occur, simply because God's word could never fail. Moriah was Abraham's virtual Calvary. Later it would be the literal historical Calvary, God's own Son our substitute. *"He who spared not His own Son, but delivered Him up for us all, how shall He not with Him freely give us all things?"* (Romans 8:32).

Faith Triumphs over Law Keeping   Romans 4: 13-16

Before the law was ever given, Paul establishes beyond question that Abraham experienced justification by faith. Now David, after the law was given and apart from the Law, testified to God's forgiveness of his sins as a believer, again by grace through faith. *"Blessed is he whose transgression is forgiven, whose sin **is covered**. Blessed is the man to whom the LORD **does not impute** iniquity, And in whose spirit there is no guile"* (Psalm 32: 1, 2; 51: 1-7). The law serves only to reveal God's holiness and his wrath toward sin, not his forgiveness of sin. Grace and faith have triumphed.

Paul in a few brief words unites the two divine principles of grace and faith in one simple statement. Paul will use the "father of faith, Abraham," to say: ***"Therefore it is of faith that it might be according to grace,*** *so that the promise might be sure to all the seed, not only those who are of the law, but also to those who are of the faith of Abraham, who is the father of us all"* (4:16).

Grace operates were faith reigns; faith operates where grace reigns. The depth of understanding of this truth is generally lost on us in terms of the Christian walk or sanctification or holy living.

We do affirm and rejoice in these two principles in our justification, our new standing in the presence of God. But with our current "works/Christian service mentality" after initial salvation, we seem to lose the uniqueness of them in the Holy Spirit's developing in us Christ-likeness, the very essence of sanctification. So often we think that our work for him adds value to our standing; service even in God's name can become a secret source of pride. But faith leaves no room for pride, the essence of sin, and grace triumphs in our weakness.

Sanctifying Faith in Abraham as Seen in the Birth of Isaac Romans 4:17-25.

If justifying faith is illustrated in his believing God in Ur at the age of 75 and older (Genesis 12:4; 15:6), this is the very same faith that operates in the sanctifying faith at age 100; for twenty five years he had faced the utter impossibility of a son on whom God's promise of universal blessing would rest (v.19). Now we see the sanctifying faith of a mature believer, trusting God just as implicitly as when he left Ur, and now much more so than ever.

Let that comparison sink in. He was no more able to justify himself in Ur than he could sanctify himself in the Promised Land. It was going to be God and only God on his terms of grace and faith. Paul is underlining the truth that simple faith is the only entrance into holiness and Christ-likeness. It must be grace plus faith plus nothing more in both justification and sanctification.

What follows is the anatomy or the analysis of faith as the Spirit describes the stages of development of Abraham's sanctifying faith.

The Resignation of Faith in Sanctification, an initial step of a tested faith   Romans 4:17, 18

In sovereign grace God waited thirteen years (Abraham's age 86-99) since his carnal dependence on Sarai and Hagar (Genesis 16); God purposely waited until every human hope had been lost for the son as promised. But God is described as one *"who gives life to the dead and calls those things which do not exist as though they did* (v.17).

God would not compromise his deeper work of sanctifying grace in Abraham, *"who, contrary to hope, in hope believed, so that he became the father of many nations, according to what was spoken."* Abraham had no other earthly option. God wants to bring us to that point of death to self and dependence on him in any sanctifying work of grace--never an easy place to accept.

L.E. Maxwell, my mentor and to whom I dedicate this book, entitled one his books: **Crowded to Christ.** So was Abraham and so must we be crowded to Christ in simple faith.

The Rejoicing of Faith in Sanctification, a maturing of tested faith   Romans 4:19, 20b

"And not being weak in faith, he did not consider his own body, already dead and the deadness of Sarah's womb." This is what faith does **NOT** do. It does not weigh the options or rate the probabilities. There is no other source from which life

can come, never from ourselves but always from him who raises the dead.

Paul also had tried once to battle his own flesh and in total defeat confesses: *"But I see another law in my members, warring against the law of my mind, and bringing me into captivity to the law of sin which is in my members. O wretched man that I am! Who will deliver me from this body of death?"* (Romans 7: 23, 24).

But Paul describes the faith of Abraham: *"He did not waver at the promise of God through unbelief, but was strengthened in faith, giving glory to God."* He will not look inside but rather to the promise of God - rejoicing follows, even when faith is not yet realized in sight.

The <u>Rest</u> of Faith in Sanctification, a mature faith Romans 4:21-25

*" . . . And being fully convinced that what He had promised He was also able to perform. And therefore 'it **was accounted** to him for righteousness.' Now it was not written for his sake alone. . . .but also for us. It shall **be imputed to us** who believe in Him who raised up Jesus our Lord from the dead"* (vv. 21-24).

It is highly significant that the very same theological language of righteousness accounted to Abraham in justification (Genesis 15: 6) is used to describe the righteousness imputed or accounted to us **NOW** in sanctification (Romans 4: 24). What a convincing proof that sanctification is by faith alone without any thing that we can do to merit it! It is God's gift to us, the gift of his son.

Notice carefully what Paul says about Abraham's experience before God; he was already a mature but still a maturing believer. This passage becomes highly relevant to our walk with God. *Paul will develop this truth in the next chapters.* Faith is a not an historical detail, but a real walk of faith grounded in the imputed righteousness of Christ, still our only standing for any subsequent walk in Christ-likeness.

Paul here links the truths of justifying faith to sanctifying faith in the person of Abraham who demonstrates for us our standing and our walk grounded in simple faith and always in God's grace. Merit and works in his name, years of service do not enter into God's equation.

Some Deductions on Faith and its Sanctifying Power

1. Paul chooses two events in Abraham's life to illustrate the role of faith in a full salvation: first in Ur of the Chaldees at 75 and in Canaan at 100 expecting the birth of Isaac.
2. Paul makes no distinction between the two events with regard to the nature of faith. God operates on the basis of grace and develops faith and dependence in his own. This speaks to the unity of God's saving work. It is his doing, resulting in a maturing faith.
3. **We have come to separate justification from sanctification, but God does not allow it.** Whom he justifies he desires to sanctify. Holiness is God's plan for the true believer.
4. The development of Abraham's faith is the prime work of God through the Holy Spirit.

Chapter 11

AN OVERVIEW OF JUSTIFICATION AND SANCTIFICATION

Romans 5:1-8

Paul has fully explained the marvel of justification, a new permanent standing for the believer who has been **declared** as righteous as Christ his savior, forgiven of all his sins and restored to a full inheritance in Christ, "*heir of God and joint heir with Christ*" (Romans 3:21-31; 8:17*).*

All this comes to the believer from the grace of God on the basis of the shed blood of Christ and by simple faith or trust in God's infallible promise. Implicit in the truth of justification is the truth of sanctification or Christ-likeness. We must not isolate justification from its expression in our daily walk. What God has joined together, let no man put asunder!

Paul will expound on the **MUCH MORE** of Christ-likeness or sanctification in Romans 5:12-21; but he pauses now to look backward and forward. He does it in a masterful fashion in Romans 5:1-8. In these verses we see the *reign of God's grace* extended to the "*ungodly who believes.*" Remember that all this inheritance comes to us gratis without works, neither merit nor demerit. Neither Christian service nor years of ministry add merit to the full enjoyment of salvation's blessings. *God's grace reigns in us.*

Seven Blessings that Flow from the Cross   Romans 5:1-6

Paul is now approaching the half-way point in this treatment of the Gospel of Christ. With a deeper grasp of the marvel of grace, Paul will pause and in these verses crisply summarize what was given to us at the Cross. He will use this as his launch pad to introduce the deeper aspects of the Cross. It is clear that Paul, in one sense, has already introduced the approaching truth of sanctification as illustrated in the life of Abraham; that truth is Paul's greatest concern. We will see a new depth to the Cross-work that will highlight the full triumph of the Cross.

A numerical summary of the verses dedicated to different topics is significant: the problem of sin = **sixty-four** verses (1:18- 3:20); justification and the exposition of faith = **forty-seven** verses (3:21-4:25); a look backward and forward = **eight** verses (5:1-8); sanctification, our new condition of death to sin, death to the law, Paul's personal failure and our walk in the Holy Spirit = **one hundred verses** (5:9-8:39).

It is important to grasp the first word of Rom. 5:1, *"Therefore"* which returns us to the previous statement: *"Who was delivered up because of our offenses, and was raised **because of** our justification"* (Romans 4:25). The last phrase is very interesting; God had so determined to accept his Son's death as full payment for sin that on that basis alone, we were declared righteous; **resurrection would follow that fact and add a new dynamic to the believer**. The risen life of Christ is now ours to claim by faith.

Paul introduces a thought seldom grasped by many that the resurrection opens up to us in full reality a new chapter in the life of the justified--*"we shall be saved by his life"* (v.10). Paul will develop this fully later in Romans 6-8, but here we see the complementary value of the resurrection. Generally the resurrection has been seen only as God ratifying and accepting his Son's death. It surely is that, but it **opens a new chapter for Christian living**--*"not I but Christ"* (Galatians 2:20; Colossians 3:3, 4; Philippians 1:21).

A Backward and Present Look--A Seven Fold Blessing Romans 5:1,2

Paul introduces the **first blessing** by using a past [aorist] passive participle, *"having being justified,"* as an act completed (4:24, 25). Nothing is pending and on the basis of that great fact, we enjoy peace with God. Some translate it: *"Let us have peace with God."* This does not weaken the fact, but only makes it more urgent that we take full advantage of it. Whether we take the statement as a past fact or an exhortatory request to live it to the full, the glorious fact remains; peace with God has been established and that once for all. Let that settle the issue of our past sins, guilt, destiny and God's full favor. Our past has been cancelled and now our present is assured.

A **second blessing** follows; we have (had) access (v. 1). That acceptance grants us full entrance into his presence. What a contrast with the Mosaic Law that prefaced the Day of Atonement with a word to Moses: *"Tell Aaron your brother not to come at simply any time into the Holy Place inside the veil"* (Leviticus 16:2). Unlimited access is now ours. *"Let us therefore come boldly to the throne of grace, that we may* *obtain mercy and find grace to help in time of need"* (Hebrews 4:16).

Do we avail ourselves of this choice privilege of access into his presence at any time? This availability of entering the Holiest of Holies is the monumental achievement of the Cross. The veil was rent in two from top to bottom. The writer to the Hebrews sums up the whole argument of his book by appealing to the reader: *"Therefore, brethren, having boldness to enter the Holiest by the blood of Jesus, by a new and living way which he consecrated for us, through the veil, that is, His flesh, and having a High Priest over the house of God, let us draw near with a true heart in full assurance of faith…"* (Hebrews 10:19-22).

A **third blessing** assures us of a firm standing in grace by faith. *"Through whom also we have access by faith into this grace in which we stand"* (v. 2). It is a standing before God not limited by time or performance. It is an unconditioned status granted by grace and sustained by obedient faith. Notice the joining of the two principles of God's Cross-work: *"Therefore, it is of faith that it might be according to grace"* (4:16). Our present is assured.

A **fourth blessing** follows. So permanent is our standing that we can *"rejoice in hope of the glory of God"* (v. 2). A future hope made secure in Christ enables us to stand today because tomorrow is guaranteed in his presence. This truth answers one of life's eternal questions: What is my future? What awaits me, condemnation or acceptance into his presence? The true believer's eternal security is established beyond any possible change. Our future is assured.

The **fifth blessing** calls for a living faith in the present! *"And not only that, but we also glory in tribulations"* (v. 3), but Paul does not stop abruptly here. He adds a shortened version of Romans 8:28. In our present walk tribulations are producing in us God's greater purposes of holiness.

The purposes of God carry us through a series of stages that run the gamut from panic, to patience, to perseverance, to character building in faith and issue in new hope on a more sure foundation of his sovereign love fashioning in us the very likeness of Christ. Jesus preceded us in every stage of temptation and trial without sin. *"For in that He Himself has suffered, being tempted, He is able to aid those who are tempted"* (Hebrews 2:18). What a consolation!

I personally saw God's turning a likely catastrophe into hope. In 1958 an internal specialist told me frankly that I had throat cancer; if it were malignant, as he expected, I would have six months to live; surgery was necessary. He told Grace that if the surgery lasted 4 hours, they would have taken my vocal cords. It came as sudden shock. I was thirty and had just begun my Spanish teaching ministry at RGBI; future ministry was therefore in great jeopardy. The human options were not good: cancer, loss of my vocal cords, and maybe I would never see the daughter my wife was carrying.

But God sustained me with the realization that God is infinitely good. Therefore, I had nothing to fear whether it be by life or by death. God gave me what the psalmist said, very much better than what I could have imagined. *"He will not be afraid of evil tidings; His heart is steadfast, trusting in the LORD. His heart is established; He will not be afraid..."* (Psalm 112:7, 8). I had to wait two weeks before surgery could be performed. I remember so distinctly that as we drove to Harlingen, Texas, Grace and I sang:

A Wonderful Saviour is Jesus my Lord.
A wonderful Saviour to me;
He hideth my soul in the cleft of the rock,
Where rivers of pleasure I see.

A Wonderful Saviour is Jesus my Lord.
He taketh my burden away;
He holdeth me up, and I shall not be moved,
He giveth me strength as my day.

He hideth my soul in the cleft of the rock,
That shadows a dry thirsty land;
He hideth my life in the depths of his love,
And covers me there with His hand,
And covers me there with his hand

Fanny Crosby 1918

The tumor was encapsulated and removed; I would still have my already nasal voice, having earlier been afflicted by polio at age sixteen. I look back on those two weeks and the fifty five years that have followed knowing that God produced in me: a measure of panic, perseverance, character and hope. I would not exchange those days for anything.

The **sixth blessing** is the love of God poured out prolifically in our hearts. Now for the very first time Paul in Romans explains the overwhelming role of God's love. Until now it has been God's wrath, but only now can we appreciate his love so graciously explained in Romans 5:6-8, verses we often share with the unbeliever. But now that love is ours to enjoy.

Until now in Romans Paul has greatly emphasized justification, our new legal position; God's love poured out is

Paul's one reference to regeneration that always accompanies justification. Regeneration is the act of God by which he imparts or gives to us eternal life, the agents being the Word of God and the Holy Spirit.

To Titus Paul writes: *"But when the kindness and the love of God our Savior toward man appeared, not by works of righteousness which we have done, but according to His mercy He saved us, through the washing of regeneration and renewing of the Holy Spirit"* (Titus 3:4,5). Regeneration gives us a new quality of life, eternal life, a new **condition** which becomes the beginning of sanctification. Paul is preparing the reader for the new main theme of Romans.

The **seventh blessing** is the capstone of grace: *"the Holy Spirit that one already having been given to us."* Paul began Rom. 5:1 with a past aorist) participle, having peace with God from the moment of justification and concludes the paragraph with the identical grammatical construction. He assures us that at that very first moment of justification and regeneration we are given the third person of the Trinity, not to be sought after but rather to be received with gratitude and to experience fully the life of Christ, now our very life.

Paul will not mention the Holy Spirit again until Romans 7: 6 by which time he will have laid out fully the truth of our identification with Christ in our death to the sin principle (Romans 6) and our death to the law, in spite of our best but fruitless efforts (Romans 7: 7-25). Then, and only then, can the Spirit do his work of revealing the Christ-life in the believer.

Notice Paul's references to the Spirit in Romans: from a single reference to the Spirit of holiness in the introduction (1:4) to the second one in Romans 5: 6, to a third one (7:6) to some 21 references to the fullness of the ministry of the Spirit in Romans 8. It is after the fullness of the Message of the Cross has been presented that the Holy Spirit is then free to reveal to the believer the **reign of God's grace** in his Son.

What an overwhelming survey of the past and the future with the present guaranteed by the love of God and the presence of the Holy Spirit! What more can we ask for?

Basic to all our walk is the precious blood of Christ which brings us nigh to a forgiving God.

Precious, precious Blood of Jesus, shed on Calvary;
Shed for rebels, shed for sinners,
Shed for thee![6]

Chorus
Precious, precious Blood of Jesus, ever flowing free;
Oh, believe it, oh, receive it,
'Tis for Thee.

Precious, precious Blood of Jesus, let it make thee whole;
Let it flow in mighty cleansing
O'er thy soul.

Though thy sins be red like crimson, deep in scarlet glow,
Jesus' precious Blood shall wash thee
Whiter as snow.

Precious Blood that hath redeemed us! All the price is paid!
Perfect pardon now is offered,

---

[6] Original hymn did not capitalize "blood", but we have done so for theological reasons, as it refers to the effective sacrificial blood of the Savior and not merely to physical plasma.

Peace is made.

Now the holiest with boldness we may enter in
For the open fountain cleanseth
From all sin.

Precious Blood! by this we conquer in the fiercest fight,
Sin and Satan overcoming
By its might.

Precious Blood, whose full atonement makes us nigh to
God!
Precious blood, our way to glory,
Praise and laud.

--Frances Ridley Havergal

Truths to be Embraced in Faith by the Believer

1. God's justifying grace leads inevitably to sanctifying grace. This is the unitary work of God's grace as seen in Christ's work on the Cross.
2. As we received the forgiveness of our sins, the first aspect of the Cross, so we must receive in simple faith the fullness of our identification in his death and resurrection. Paul's statement is clear: *"As you have therefore received Christ Jesus the Lord, so walk in Him"* (Colossians 2: 6). Saved by faith and sanctified by faith, not by works.
3. While God has forgiven our past and assures us of the future, he designs to work most deeply in our present

life in Him. He has made the fullest of provision in the outpouring of his love and the gift of the Holy Spirit.

4. God produces true holiness in the crucible of suffering and tribulation. We learn to depend on him and walk by faith and not by sight. (Romans 5:3, 4; Hebrews 12: 1-11).

5. In this overview of the Christian life, you may notice the absence of our doing. **It is rather His have done what he did at the Cross and our believing the Message of the Cross that will issue in victory.**

6. We have all too often made the Christian life our doing, reading, praying, tithing, witnessing. The results have been meager, if not absent. The Christian life is ***Christ in us the hope of glory***. We return to the emphasis of the Cross, our death and our risen life in Christ.

Chapter 12

THE BRIDGE FROM ADAM TO THE RISEN LIFE OF CHRIST

Romans 5: 9-12

Paul is now prepared to launch the next major aspect of the truth of the Cross. The foundation is now well in place: the grace of God, the power of the shed blood and the role of faith, that divine/human element that issues in spiritual reality. In a seamless manner Paul makes the doctrine of justification the foundation for our sanctification. *"For no other foundation can anyone lay than that which is laid, which is Jesus Christ"* (1 Corinthians 3:11).

About the same time that Paul was writing to Rome, he was writing to the Galatians with all the passion and deep concern of a spiritual father as indeed he was. In Romans, however, he approaches the same subject matter in essence, but he does it theologically, logically and chronologically. J. B Lightfoot lists some 27 specific verses common to both epistles but related so differently according to the need of the readers.[7]

In Romans Paul gives the truths of God's grace in order of personal experience: first he presents the nucleus of the gospel in Romans 1:16, 17; then his exposé of sin is devastating (1:18-3:20). Having shown the absolute

---

[7] J.B. Lightfoot, *Epistle to the Galatians*, (London: Macmillan and Co.), 7th edition, 1881, pp. 45-48.

bankruptcy the human heart, Paul introduces the marvelous grace of God in propitiation and justification (3:21-31); he follows the gospel truths with the role of saving faith in receiving God's favor in pardon and spiritual maturity as seen in Abraham and David (4:1-29), and lastly he introduces the believer into the riches of his new inheritance (5:1-5).

Overview of the Greatness of God's Love   Romans 5:6-9

Before Paul moves on to unfold the marvel of grace in sanctification or Christ-likeness, he sums up in retrospect God's love as the ultimate moving dynamic of his "*so great salvation.*" Until now he has majored on God's justice and wrath against sin. He has not mentioned God's love until he had spelled out in clearest terms the wonder of our new standing in righteousness before God the Judge. He has unveiled the grace of God, the shedding of blood, the ransom paid and the role of faith in receiving God's forgiveness and our full restoration. We have a **new position** or standing, secure and eternal.

Until now God's love has been held, as it were, in reserve until he has presented the doctrine of regeneration which always accompanies justification. "*The love of God has been poured out in our hearts by the Holy Spirit who was given to us*" (v: 5). Ours is now a **new moral condition**, the beginning of sanctification.

In the short span of three verses Paul synthesizes in magnificent terms the desperation of our alienation, the uniqueness of his love and the unveiling of God's mercy in the person of his son. "*For when we were still without strength, in due time Christ died for the ungodly. For scarcely for a righteous man will one die; yet perhaps for a good man* someone would even dare to die. But God demonstrates His own love toward us, in that while were still sinners, Christ died of us" (vv. 6-8).

Human love may prove heroic as in the mother who dies to give birth and the soldier who dies for his country. But the extent of God's love has never ever been equalled before. His love and divine justice met at the Cross. The Psalmist said it best: *"Mercy and truth have met together; righteousness and peace have kissed each other. Truth shall spring out of the earth, and righteousness shall look down from heaven"* (Psalm 85:10, 11).

A Bridge to Paul's New Passion-Christ in Us the Hope of Glory Romans 5:9-11

We are overwhelmed to read the conclusion of that magnificent love revealed at Calvary. Could there be anything more marvelous? Our reaction would be: Nothing could ever eclipse that love at Calvary. But Paul has only begun to explore the height and depth of our new standing before God in saving grace. Calvary will prove to have new depths yet to be explored and heights to ascend.

We need to prepare ourselves for the profound reasoning of the Holy Spirit through Paul. What follows in Romans 5 will tax our logic and thinking powers but not our hearts' response to the even deeper wonder of our identification with Christ at Calvary.

While what follows may not be easy reading to the casual reader, it will yield its treasures to the earnest believer. It seems seldom, if ever, we have heard sermons on this portion before us. No wonder these truths are the "Lost Symphony" as Dr. Huegel so often said.

Allow me a word of explanation. As we proceed into the next few chapters, one may feel that I have repeated and reviewed too often the evident. In one sense I do apologize and in another sense I don't. So seldom are these truths presented that repetition will be the "mother of learning." I never cease to marvel at the *"Reign of Grace."*

By means of an argument irresistible in logic, he makes two contrasts based on a spiritual progression (vv.9-11); Paul establishes first a proven premise and then builds upon it to project a yet more far reaching result. We call it a "a fortiori" argument, that is to say, the logical force of a now proven premise that as a given leads to something even greater.

This argument can be identified often by several key words or phrases followed by a result never to be questioned: the little word *"if"* followed by a conclusion **much more**, implying from a lesser to a greater. After the magnificent presentation of God's love in his son's vicarious death (vv.6-8), he says, in effect, there is yet a result far greater that follows in strict logic. He will greatly enlarge Calvary's work of grace. This thought may challenge us.

*"**Much more** then, having now been justified by His blood, we shall be saved from wrath through Him."* We cannot question this established fact. God's wrath fell on him and none remains for me.

> "My sin--oh, the bliss of this glorious thought--
> My sin--not in part but the whole,--
> Is nailed to the cross and I bear it no more;
> Praise the Lord, praise the Lord, O my soul.
> It is well with my soul...It is well...It is well with my soul.

> Horace G. Stafford

Chapter 12: The bridge from Adam to the risen life of Christ

By means of a sound argument Paul reasons tightly: the shed blood has spoken peace forever. There can be no future wrath; his grace and his blood are proof of our eternal standing. Our future is forever eternally secure. We did nothing to merit such acceptance; he did it all at the Cross. We stand justified fully by his blood. But he still says: "**MUCH MORE**". In this equation the future peace far outweighs the cancelled wrath of God.

Now Paul introduces the next great concept upon which the remainder of Romans 5:12-8:39 is wholly based: *For if when we were enemies we were reconciled to God through the death of His Son,* **much more,** *having been reconciled, we shall be **saved by His life**"* (v.10). Reflect on Paul's statement.

Let us parse this statement to grasp its full sweep and application. Since we were enemies and now are reconciled by his vicarious death, the first premise was well established earlier; there is yet another greater premise. Since his death accomplished our reconciliation for eternity, what does now his resurrection now entail? Paul asserts in full confidence the greater result: *"We shall be saved by his life."* Paul had, in fact, already anticipated in Romans 4: 19-25 the mature faith of Abraham who saw the resurrection entailed in his virtual Calvary experience in Genesis 22.

Christ's sinless life is not the issue. In the context, it is his **risen life** now available to us in ways in which Paul will soon enter. This is the new concept, a new resource for "the just who live by faith." The Christian life becomes nothing less than the **risen life of Christ** lived out in our lives by the Holy Spirit. His vicarious death is the ground of our justification (v.9); the risen life of Christ is the ground of our sanctification.

In one sentence Paul has projected the truth of how that glorious union becomes ours.

This truth is the new point of departure that Romans 6-8 will develop, first with our death to sin (6:2) and our death to the Law (7:4) and then the work of the Holy Spirit (8:1-13). Paul has erected the bridge that spans the full reconciliation and reason for rejoicing. *"And not only that, but we also rejoice in God through our Lord Jesus Christ, through whom we have now received the reconciliation"* (v.12).

You will notice the two-fold repetition of the **much more** and then finally **not only . . . but also** stating the second aspect of his resurrection: 1) Christ for us, he died in our place, and 2) Christ in us and we in him; he lives in us.

We have become so accustomed to his death as the evidence of God's love that we generally fail to grasp the second aspect in its clarity and wonder. Paul's passion introduces us to the second and equally important aspect of his resurrection. We are now joined to him in his death and resurrection that will produce in us by the Holy Spirit nothing more nor less than the very risen life of the Crucified and Resurrected Christ in us by faith. Here in a nut shell is the *"reign of grace"* in the believer.

Our Solidarity with the Last Adam--Our Break with the First Adam   Romans 5:12-14

Our grasp of the truths of Romans 5:12-21 is key to the understanding the Magna Carta of Christian victory in Romans 6:1-14. Paul leaves no stone unturned; he returns to the actual historical original sin of the first Adam. Paul will face squarely the sin nature that we inherited in Adam and that still persists in the believer.

Chapter 12: The bridge from Adam to the risen life of Christ

Theologians may debate the "when" of sin's entrance, but 5:12 Paul states an unavoidable reality. **"Therefore, just as through one man sin entered the world, and death through sin, and thus death spread to all men, because all sinned."**

It may seem strange that Paul compares Christ with Adam considering the tragic difference and consequences that came to us in the first Adam. Jesus stated it tersely in his conversation with Nicodemus where the sharp difference between the two worlds can be seen. *"That which is born of the flesh is flesh, and that which is born of the Spirit is spirit. Do not marvel that I said to you, You must be born again"* (John 3: 6, 7).

Paul further enlarges on this reality. *"And so it is written, 'The first man Adam became a living being.' The last Adam became a life-giving spirit. . . .The first man was of the earth, made of dust; the second Man is the Lord from heaven"* (1 Corinthians 15: 45, 47). We see again the sharp contrast of the first Adam and the Last Adam: *"Therefore, if anyone is in Christ, he is a new creation; old things have passed away; behold all things have become new"* (2 Corinthians 5:17).

After having stated when sin entered, Paul now involves the sinner in that very act of Adam. Paul has affirmed without apology that *"thus death spread to all men, **because all sinned."*** Theologians may argue the nuances of this truth but the fact remains. Death spread to all men. Cemeteries are proof of that reality. The next statement is profound.

There is a vital solidarity in the human race. Our unique relationship to Adam involved us in his sin every bit as much as he in his own sin. He is the federal head of an earthly race. We were not there physically, but we were there collectively in him. The persistence of the sin nature is evident in the earliest days of a child's life. No parent has ever had to teach the youngest to lie or to demand his own will and way.

To establish the solidarity of the human race, Paul will make two stark contrasts (vv.15, 16) and three comparisons (vv.17-21) with the first Adam who sinned and infected the whole human race. The Last Adam triumphed and established a new spiritual race. The first Adam universally brought condemnation upon us all. None can deny that sad reality (Romans 3:20).

Paul's argument is that in the same way Christ's death has provided a universal provision for a new race with this one important exception. We inherited Adam's nature through no choice of our own; the new nature in Christ is offered to those who **receive** his forgiveness. *"For if by the one man's offense death reigned through the one, **much more those who receive abundance of grace and of the gift of righteousness** will reign in life through the One, Jesus Christ"* (v.17). This is NOT universal salvation, but rather a gracious provision for all who will believe.

Paul is laying the ground work for the indwelling life of Christ in us. The Christian life is not an uneasy truce or contest between the two natures, our sad past and the hope for a future betterment. There is a **much more** dimension that gives hope and confidence that Christ has conquered the power of sin and will to do that in every believer. *"Being confident of this very thing, that He who has begun a good work in you will complete it until the day of Jesus Christ"* (Philippians 1:6).

Powerful Principles to Ponder

1. Paul is going to return to the very essence of the sin problem. He will not gloss over the reality of a sin nature, a sinful dynamic in every human being.

2. Paul will show that God has made an effective provision for the believer who still must face a potential inward struggle, the inertia and the dynamic of the sin principle.

3. He will do it, however, without any concession whatsoever as to its power and right to reign in the life of the believer.

Chapter 13

THE BRIDGE TO THE RISEN LIFE OF CHRIST IN THE BELIEVER

Romans 5: 13-21

In *The Bridge from Adam to the Risen Life of Christ,* Paul laid the foundation for the next major advance in his presentation of the gospel in all of its fullness (Romans 5:9-11) After our perfect standing of being fully justified before a holy and gracious God, the problem of sins (plural) had been solved. But much remains to be learned in everyday reality; ***the problem of the sin nature and the power of that nature must be understood by the believer, not justified and defended by word or gesture***. Paul's greater concern now is the basis or the "how" of sanctification or daily Christ-likeness.

Paul traces the sin problem back to its very historic roots: *"Therefore just as through one man sin entered the world, and death through sin, and thus death spread to all men, because all sinned"* (Romans 5:12). What or who would be the remedy for this urgent problem? Paul sets forth the first Adam as the federal head of a sinful race that involved all of us in death and condemnation.

But now, Christ, the Last Adam, is the federal head or representative of a new spiritual race. As strange as this comparison of the two federal heads may be to us, the failure of the first Adam and the triumph of the Last Adam, Paul will make his case abundantly clear.

A Series of Contrasts and Comparisons--the Theological Answer   Romans 5:15-18

What could be more different than Adam and Christ? One failed miserably to obey God; Christ on the contrary heard on several occasions: *"This is my beloved son, in whom I am well pleased"* (Matthew 3:17; 17:5; John 12: 28). Paul has made it abundantly clear that while we were born in sin and of necessity born into the Adamic race with its attendant death and condemnation, we are now no longer in Adam.

We are in Christ. Our new standing is clearly outlined in Romans 5:1-6: the sevenfold blessing of peace, access, standing in grace, hope, tribulations that produce Christlike character, the love of God shed abroad in our heart and finally the Holy Spirit is our seal and gift.

We have experienced a birth from above, a radical re-birth; we are new creatures in Christ. *"Strengthened with all might, according to His glorious power, for all patience and longsuffering with joy; giving thanks to the Father who has qualified us to be partakers of the inheritance of the saints in the light. He has delivered us from the power of darkness and translated us into the kingdom of the Son of His love in whom we have redemption through His blood, the forgiveness of sins"* (Colossians 1:12-14).

This is who we are now. ***This truth must be grasped in faith before we can proceed farther.***

Paul's reasoning may appear complex. I have heard almost no sermons preached on this passage, but it is truly foundational to the truths of Romans 6 that will engage us at the deepest level of our spiritual need.

After the declaration of the entrance of sin and death and our having sinned in Adam (v.12), Paul justifies the comparison between the two very distinctly different federal heads. Prior to the law having been given by Moses, death reigned. *"Nevertheless death reigned from Adam to Moses, even over those who had not sinned according to the likeness of the transgression of Adam, **who is a type of Him who is to come"** (v.14)

The last phrase is the key that opens up to us the following verses. Adam, as much of a failure as he was, was the head of a sinful race. However, his headship was a type of Christ who was to come and would usher in a new race, spiritual and holy. Adam was a type of Christ to come and Christ the anti-type, the head of a very different race about to come.

Two Contrasts in Sharp Relief   Romans 5:15, 16

We face the sharp contrast between Adam, the failure, and Christ, the Victor. *"But the free gift is not like the offense. For if by the one man's offence many died, **MUCH MORE** the grace of God and the gift by the one Man, Jesus Christ abounded unto many* (v.15). Notice the abrupt contrast: the guilty offense versus the gracious gift. The ambience of these two realities could not be greater in depth: guilt that remains to accuse us as opposed to our rejoicing on receiving the bounty of a gift. These two concepts cannot coexist in terms of our standing before God.

One man brought ruin, the other Man the gift of grace. The similarity is that it was wrought by one man, yet Christ was so diametrically different and greater than Adam. In Adam the offense brought us condemnation and death and in the other Man grace abounded to us. But throughout these verses the **MUCH MORE** resonates for the third time.

Notice the frequency of the **MUCH MORE**, the verb to **abound** and to **reign.** These key words will unite Paul's presentation and show the superlative nature of Christ's headship in sharp contrast with First Adam's inheritance, the sin principle that persists in the believer. Do you grasp the power of this truth? What Christ brings to the believer is a gift of grace, never ever based on our merit or performance.

The second contrast: *"And the gift is not like that which came through the one who sinned. For the judgment which came from one offense resulted in condemnation, but the free gift which came from many offenses resulted in justification"* (v.16). The point of the contrast is powerful: one man brought death and condemnation to all but the free gift - a blessed redundancy - from the other Man brought full vindication and justification to all. One condemned all and one freed all. Could anything be more different?

Three Comparisons Complete the Cycle   Romans 5:17-19

Paul pursues the realities of two distinct headships, the First Adam and the Last Adam and highlights some points of comparison but always with the absolute superiority of the **MUCH MORE** of Christ.

In the first comparison Paul returns to his "a fortiori argument": *"For **if** by the one man's offence death reigned through the one, **MUCH MORE** those who **receive abundance of grace** and of the **gift** of righteousness will **reign in life** through the One, Jesus Christ"* (v.17). Earlier the contrasts highlighted the difference in the end results: in Adam guilt, in

Christ a free gift (v.15), in Adam condemnation, in Christ justification.

The three comparisons will highlight the similarities with contrasting results: 1) The offense of one, from Adam to many that led to death. In Christ from one Man, Christ, to many reigning in life *"having received the abundance of grace and of the gift of righteousness"* (v.17). 2) The offense of one, Adam to condemnation, in Christ to justification (v.18). 3) The disobedience in Adam to the many being sinners, the obedience in Christ to many being declared righteous. What contrasts and comparisons!

Paul advances the argument by underscoring the value of words repeatedly used: the **abundance of grace,** no meager store, a repetition of the **gift** of grace and the believer **reigning** right now in union with Christ. To reign in life is now the heritage of very believer declared righteous in Christ.

Verse 17 is really the capstone of the whole argument. The believer is never to be a victim to the presence of the old nature. Rather he receives by faith the abundance of grace and the gift of righteousness. The verb to "receive" returns the believer back to his initial act of faith. John had said: *"But to as many as received Him, He gave the right to become children of God, even to those who believe on His name"* (John 1:12). The truth of that verse introduced me to my salvation at the age of 12.

In the second comparison (v.18) Paul has stated the fullness of our identification with Christ or our new head. He sums up the comparison of the two federal heads as applying equally to all men. But earlier (v.17) he also adds a limiting fact, because it might appear that from the verse that follows that he taught a universal salvation. *"Therefore, as though one* man's offense judgment came to all men, resulting in condemnation, even so through one Man's righteous act the free gift came to all men, resulting in justification of life (v.18)."

At first reading it might be thought that as all sinned in Adam, so all are justified in Christ. But this verse must be taken in the context of the limiting factor clearly stated in the preceding verse (v.17), that is: *"those who receive abundance of grace and the gift of righteousness will reign in life."*

In the third comparison Paul restates the same truth for emphasis. *"For as by one man's disobedience many were made sinners, so also by one Man's obedience many will be made righteous"* (v.19). Clearly this was all accomplished at the Cross by his judicial obedience to God credited to our account. From our previous status of sinners, God declares us to being as righteous as his own Son.

Limits of the Law and the Reign of Grace   Romans 5:20, 21

Sin is activated and energized by the law. *"For by the law is the knowledge of sin"* (3: 20). But the law's last word cannot stand in the face of God's grace. *"But where sin abounded, grace abounded MUCH MORE, so that as sin reigned in death, even so grace might reign through righteousness to eternal life though Jesus Christ our Lord"* (5:21). Paul uses the verb to say "if sin abounded and indeed it did in Adam, but God's grace super abounded," the fifth **MUCH MORE.**

Notice carefully in v. 21 it is not we who reign--we saw that in verse17--but rather its **God's grace that reigns in us.** Whatever victory could be ours is his, never ours. And it is victory, not found in miracles and signs and wonders, but in Christ's righteousness, ***saved by his life*** (v.10). The signs of that true righteousness in us will be holiness and humility and love.

A New Focus and a New Reality Awaits the Believer in Christ

Even a cursory reading of the "a fortiori" arguments of Paul underlines several realities that faith must grasp. Five times in thirteen verses Paul says: **MUCH MORE** (9, 10, 15, 17, 21). Nothing the Adamic nature brings to the believer can ever stand in the way of the *dúnamis*--power of the Gospel to transform life and conduct.

Furthermore, the two verbs resonate throughout the passage *"to abound"* and *"to reign in life"*. There is nothing niggardly or meager about the outcome. The Christian life lived in the power of the gospel must be nothing less than a triumphant life. Resources in Christ abound in spite of any inherent evil our nature may bring. This has a powerful impact on whatever may be our genetic inheritance or our family tree. We cannot blame our past for the failures of our walk. No past can impair our future. We are in Christ.

A Practical Reality to Be Grasped in Faith

If Paul teaches us anything in this chapter it is that nothing, absolutely nothing that we inherited in Adam, is too much for a risen Christ who lives in the believer. Psychology has made so much of the influence of the past that, in effect, tends to belittle our standing in Christ. As if, little if anything can be done to remedy it. Christian counselors have often "bought into" that concept and suggest that much depends on personal effort. But *"where sin abounded, grace abounded much more."*

Our present culture treats homosexuality, lesbianism and transgender as a given, inherited from birth itself and virtually immune to change. In coming days when many more are saved out of that culture and mindset, we must be scripturally grounded in the truth that in Christ we are new creatures. No doubt there will be tensions to face between that mindset with its past permissive attitude and the truths of Scriptures. But the practical reality is that Christ triumphed over our sinful nature at the Cross.

One Last Pronouncement of Our Solidarity with a Risen Christ   Romans 5:20-21

How deeply we need to lay hold of the truth of our absolute oneness with Christ. A new position in justification becomes a new condition in sanctification. We can never doubt our past tragic relationship with Adam. Sickness, death and sin are the inevitable facts of life. But Paul is actually saying **MUCH MORE** is the surety of our present relationship with Christ. Once again Paul's arguments lend full reason to faith that will lead to the blessed reality of Romans 6 through 8.

Now and only now are we prepared to answer the immediate question of Romans 6: 1: *"What shall we say then? Shall we continue to sin that grace may abound? Certainly not! How shall **we who died to sin** live any longer in it?"* This will bring us to our understanding of victory, the reigning life in Christ.

Powerful Points to Ponder

1. The dynamic of justification is the blood of Christ shed for the remission of sins (Romans 5:9), while the

dynamic of sanctification is the risen life of Christ (Romans 5: 10).

2. The overriding message of Romans 5:12-21 is the **MUCH MORE** of Christ's work and our oneness with him in that death and resurrection process.

3. We can no more readily doubt our connection with fallen Adam than we can doubt our solidarity with Christ. That oneness is the anchor of our walk of faith.

4. The Christian life cannot be an uneasy truce between the first Adam and the Last Adam. The Christian life can never be defined as a struggle in the face of our resources in Christ.

5. Our new **position** in justification is now undergirded by our new standing in a Risen Christ which will issue in a new **condition,** the vital sharing in his death and risen life.

Chapter 14

THE BELIEVER'S NEW POINT OF DEPARTURE

Romans 6:1-6

In Paul's treatment of our being in the Last Adam, in Christ (Romans 5:12-21), he brings us to our true point of departure that leads to real victory in Christ. Of course, it is a walk by faith, but it has its specific point of departure, its process and its steps toward a truly life-changing experience in the risen Christ.

On a later occasion Paul characteristically expresses this victory in the terms of life and service. *"Yet in all these things we are more than conquerors through Him who loved us"* (Romans 8:37). And once again: *"Now thanks be to God who **always** leads us in **triumph** in Christ, and through us diffuses the fragrance of His knowledge **in every place"*** (2 Corinthians 2:14).

This is not smoke and mirrors. There is a victory that is real, practical and available within the reach of every child of God. It may not be immediate or automatic, but it has a beginning, a growth and in the end what truly glorifies our Savior.

Our Standing in the Last Adam--We Died to the Sin Principle
Romans 6:1, 2

In the preceding passage of Romans 5:12-21, Paul has been at pains to affirm that in the First Adam we inherited a sin nature incorrigible and debased; in effect we *"were dead in trespasses and sins"* (Ephesians 2:1). But now we stand alive in him, fully identified with the Last Adam (1 Corinthians 15: 45-49).

The good news is that we share the very death and life of Christ at the superlative level of **MUCH MORE** (Romans 5: 9; 10, 15, 17, 20). *"If anyone is in Christ, he is a new creation; old things have passed away; behold, all things have become new"* (2 Corinthians 5:17). The true Christian life is not a struggle that ends in an unsatisfactory standoff. *"There remains therefore a rest for the people of God"* (Hebrews 4:9). If there are difficulties, they are of our own making.

A Pertinent Question that Begs an Answer   Romans 6:1

Paul now builds upon the five MUCH MORE of Romans 5 that resonate in the superlative union that is now ours in Christ, the Head of a new spiritual race. There is no break in Paul's line of reasoning, sometimes a little difficult to follow, but oh! so vital to grasp the truths that follow. He has just stated that *"even so* **grace** *might* **reign** *through righteousness to eternal life through Jesus Christ our Lord"* (5:21).

He asks: What does the normal Christian life look like in real life? He poses the question: Shall we keep on sinning so God in his abundant grace will continue to forgive us? His answer is stunningly clear: Perish such a thought. There can be no equivocation, no delay in his response.

Paul surprises us with the answer he gives. It is not what we might expect - No, we should not sin. But rather we are taken aback by his stark but logical response. **"How** shall we who **died to sin** live any longer in it?" Such a course of action would be wholly inconsistent with the new reality of our death to sin in Christ. It would mean an outright denial of the virtue of Christ's judicial death.

That critical verb, "How shall we who **died to sin** live any longer in it?" [an aorist or past tense] was a judicial death, a death in our representative that occurred at Calvary, once for all, never to be repeated. It is now the **Point of Departure** for our walk of faith.

The parallel is abundantly clear: I sinned in Adam and death resulted; I died in Christ and risen life results in me. Now we remember that earlier key phrase: "much more having been reconciled, we shall be saved by his [risen] life" (5:10). The fact that we did die in Christ may seem difficult to grasp.

Here is where faith enters in. Paul reminds us: "As you have therefore received Christ Jesus the Lord, so walk in Him" (Colossians 2:6). In the very same way when we first heard the gospel: Christ died for you, you trusted him. Now at this juncture of the Christian walk, the same God says: you died in my Son's death to sin. We believed the first, why cannot we believe the second truth?

What Does our Death in Him Signify?--We Died to Sin Romans 6:1, 2

In the last analysis, I cannot explain it because its vital meaning depends on your "hearing of faith" (Galatians 3: 2, 5) and the exclusive work of the Holy Spirit. But I am quick to add; the Holy Spirit will illumine your heart, given your openness to hear and obey.

First, it does not mean that sin died to you. The innate power of the old life remains in our mortal bodies, but there is a big **BUT.** The essence of death is *separation,* not non-existence or eradication. In Christ's death God separated us from the power, the tyranny of the old life and set us free.

This was a once and for all act that took place at the Cross 2000 years ago. But the Holy Spirit will make it operative in you on the conditions of simple faith and obedience. The same believing faith that brought salvation in the first place, in grace will bring you victory over that old persistent sin nature.

We died with respect to the power and control of the old nature. This is a God fact and must be believed on the strength of his character. He says it. We may not "feel" it in terms of an experience, but nor did our salvation depend our "feeling saved" at any given point in the past. We have accepted that Christ died for us; now we learn the other side of the divine coin. We died in Christ's death and he lives in us; the two go hand in hand.

This Vital Truth Carefully Analyzed and Synthesized Romans 6:3-5

Because the truth of our death with Christ is so seldom preached or sung about in our hymns, it may seem strange to our evangelical ears. My mentor Dr. F. J. Huegel used to say: "Romans 6 is the gospel for Christian believers." (I can't resist the Spanish: "Romanos 6 es el <u>evangelio</u> para los <u>evangélicos</u>.")

In the following verses the Holy Spirit breaks down this truth in three concise statements. In the first one Paul uses one of his customary rhetorical questions when showing surprise that something so fundamental as our death in Christ has not been fully grasped. *"Or do you not know that as many of us as were baptized into Christ Jesus were baptized into His death?"* (v.3). The preposition "into" is equivalent to "unto" or "in" and is used in Galatians 3:27 where it refers to putting on an outward garment or uniform[8].

The thought of baptism is not a direct reference to the Biblical ordinance but rather the thought of a vital identification. The baptism is a direct reference to Paul's foundational truth of our becoming a member of the Body of Christ, a Spirit baptism. *"For **by one Spirit we were all baptized into one body** -- whether Jews of Greeks, whether slaves or free -- and have all been made to drink into one Spirit"* (1 Corinthians 12: 13). In the moment of conversion or justification we immediately became a member of the mystical Body of Christ, he the Head and we the members. The baptism does not refer to any subsequent experience.

The essence of two of the verbs (vv.3, 4) is in the passive voice, an action done to us and we the recipients and an aorist or past tense. We were baptized into his death. And to follow up on that, Paul adds: *"Therefore we were buried with Him through baptism into death, that just as Christ was raised from the dead by the glory of the Father, even so we also should walk in newness of life"* (v.4). Paul is at pains to refer us to our union with Christ in his death, burial and resurrection. The resultant reality is newness of life. The verbal thrust of

---

[8] A. T. Robertson, *Word Pictures in the New Testament* (Nashville, TN. Broadman Press), Volume IV, 1931. p.361.

"newness" is not merely a relative change but rather a new quality of life, a new source of life.

Paul now will change the time frame of the verb: *"For if we have been united together in the likeness of His death, certainly we also shall be in the likeness of His resurrection"* (v.5). I will give my paraphrase of the original; since *we have become grown together* in the likeness of his death, so shall we also be in the likeness of his resurrection. This is a first class condition assuming that which is true;[9] His adding certainly means that there can be no breakdown in the chain of his death, burial, resurrection and our being brought into that full identification with him. There is a point of departure --our death to sin--but also a **process** to fruit bearing in sharing his risen life.

The Christian life, then, has its point of departure in a spiritual grafting of us into the very life of a Crucified and Risen Christ. All that he experienced is now ours by virtue of his doing and our union with him. Jesus shared that truth with his disciples in the Upper Room Discourse. *"Abide in me, and I in you. As the branch cannot bear fruit of itself, unless it abides in the vine, neither can you, unless you abide in Me. I am the vine, you are the branches. He who abides in Me, and I in him, bears **much fruit**; for without Me you can do nothing"* (John 15: 4, 5).

Jesus had earlier made mention of "**much fruit**" In John 12: 24-26: *"Most assuredly, I say to you, unless a grain of wheat falls into the ground and dies, it remains alone; but if it dies, it produces much grain. He who loves his life will lose it, and he who hates his life in this world will keep it for eternal life."*

---

[9] Ibid, p.362.

Christ himself was __THE__ grain of wheat.[10] His unique death guaranteed the coming of the Greeks. But Jesus would never see them in the flesh, but his followers as individual grains of wheat would die and bear much fruit.   Jesus envisions his followers as being those who hated their life and would be honored by his Father just as he was.

Instead of an exclusive reference to our death in Christ at the Cross in the past (vv.2-4), Paul adds the **process** of planting a seed, allowing it to die, waiting for its first shoot and later growth (v.5).

I see this as the **process,** the walk of faith, based on the eternal fact of our once and for all death in Christ -- our new **Point of Departure.**

Powerful Truths to Be Grasped

1. God states categorically that we died to sin (6:2); therefore we need not sin constantly. There has been a cosmic blow dealt to the old sin nature.
2. Death to sin does not mean sin's non-existence or destruction, but rather God has created an effective separation in the realm of sin's power and tyranny over the believer.
3. God's himself executed these acts that are truths for us to receive and believe.
4. With this new **Point of Departure** we can in full faith begin our walk of faith, *"As you have therefore received Christ Jesus the Lord, so walk in Him"* (Colossians 2: 6).
5. Romans 6:2 states categorically that we died with reference to sin's power. This is God's judicial

---

[10] A. T. Robertson, *Word Pictures in the New Testament* (Nashville, TN: Broadman Press), Volume V, 1931. pp. 225, 226.

pronouncement, but there is much more to follow in Romans 6-8.

Chapter 15

THE KEY VERSE – THE PROCESS OF *"KNOWING THIS"*

Romans 6:6

Paul has set forth the new **Point of Departure.** It is God's radical solution for the Adamic nature, the flesh, the "ego". It is nothing less than: *"How shall we who **died to sin** live any longer in it?"* (Romans 6: 1). This is God's final verdict on the sin principle with regard to his justified ones. By one stroke, in the death of the Last Adam, he ended the power of the sin nature in us. He did not consult with us, nor ask our permission.

God knew that the "old man" was incorrigible and totally beyond repair. His plan was to displace its power and **graciously** give in its place the risen life of his Son through the Holy Spirit given once and for all. The Christian life would be the process of **knowing** God's judgment as absolutely necessary. Please notice the key verb--**knowing** (Romans 6:6).

The Masterful Summation of the Point of Departure Romans 6:2-5

In our previous study of Romans 6:1-5 we learned that God uses four verses to explain to our doubting hearts the truth and the reality of our judicial death with Christ on the cross some 2000 years ago. That judicial death seems to defy our understanding at first sight. But the truth is rooted in Romans

5:12-21 where God establishes the sad fact that in the First Adam's sin we were directly implicated in his death and condemnation. No one can deny that reality. In the same way but **MUCH MORE** in the Last Adam, Christ, we were implicated directly in his death and resurrection.

In brief summary we were baptized by one Spirit into the Body of Christ at the moment of justification and regeneration (1 Corinthians 12:13). That Spirit baptism is now pictured in the ordinance of water baptism. It becomes a public testimony to our assent to having died to the past and now we live unto God (v.3). Burial inevitably is followed by resurrection and newness of life (v.4).

The word "new" ["kainotes" in Greek] means: "renewal, not simply an experience similar to the past, but a **qualitatively different one.**"[11] That new quality of life is *Christ in us the hope of glory* (Colossians 1:27). We "have been grown together, being planted" in the likeness of death, it follows inevitably that we shall be now in the likeness of his resurrection (v.5).

The key verse: Romans 6:6

"knowing this"

There is a world of meaning in this single verse. This vital verb is a gerund that states ongoing action from the time frame already established--the Cross. No end is envisioned. The action of the verb becomes an ongoing process. The verb in the original "ginosko"[12] is "to *know experientially* as contrasted to know intuitively, thinking, reflecting upon,

---

[11] Spiros Zodhiates, *The Complete Word Study Dictionary*: New Testament, (Chattanooga, TN, AMG Publishers), 1992, p.805.

[12] Ibid, p. 898.

being mindful of." This is not academic knowledge or theological dogma or acquired information but rather a truth to be experienced, lived and more fully grasped. It infers an illumination from without, an illumination of the Spirit, resulting in an ever more profound grasp of its meaning.

In Spanish in which I am very conversant as a grammar teacher for more than fifty years, we have two verbs that are of very different in range and usage. One verb is "saber" to know a fact, to know about something. Columbus discovered America in 1492. It is data. It has no direct emotional or relational impact on the speaker.

The other verb "conocer" covers the meaning of the Greek verb, "ginosko." In Spanish it is used almost exclusively of a relationship with a person and is charged in Hispanic or Latin culture with all the highly personal knowledge and/or friendship. It can infer a longstanding and highly valued friendship, often involving an "abrazo" (a hug) and kiss on the cheek. It is affective, emotional, relational resulting in confidence and "cariño" (affection). It can also be used of a place, if one refers to the place of his birth where he knows firsthand the hidden by ways and childhood haunts, an in depth personal knowledge.

The corresponding verb in Hebrew is "yadha" meaning to perceive, understand, to be acquainted with a woman in a sexual way. It may also describe a personal knowledge of God.[13] The verb in Hebrew is used in Genesis 4:1: *"And Adam knew Eve his wife, and she conceived and bore Cain and said: 'I have gotten a man from the LORD.'"*

---

[13] Dr. Spiros Zodhiates, The Complete Word Study Old Testament, (Chattanooga,TN: AMG Publishers), 1994, p.2321.

With this etymology we can see the depth of meaning invested in our relationship with Christ. Marriage becomes a figure of the true: *"for we are members of His body, of His flesh and of His bones"* (Ephesians 5: 30, 32).

Such a spiritual knowledge comes through a humbling experience and encounter with a holy God and the convicting power of the Holy Spirit. ***"Knowing this"*** is a direct reference to the full experiential grasp of Romans 6: 1-4: identification in his death, burial and resurrection and being grown together in his likeness and *"made to sit in heavenly places in Christ Jesus"* (Ephesians 2:6).

The reference is specifically to our having died with Christ (v.6). This knowing comes to us by the Spirit's dealings in our lives and his illumination (Ephesians 1:15-20) marked by a hunger and thirst for righteousness (Matthew. 5:6).

The key verse: Romans 6:6

"that our old man was crucified with Him"

The **Point of Departure** is restated as the object of our knowing our identification with Christ in death to sin and resurrection life. Paul has identified the "old man" as all that in Adam has come down to us by our birth, having being born in sin and inherently confirmed by our choices and actions. Paul has often contrasted and compared the old with the New. He has dedicated Romans 5:12-21 to the treatment in his fivefold insistence on the **MUCH MORE** in Christ.

Usually Paul uses the term "flesh" as a reference to the old nature. In Ephesians 4:23, 24: *"And be renewed in the spirit of your mind, and that you put on the new man which was created according to God, in righteousness and true holiness."* In Philippians 3:3 he defines the believer: *"For we are the* circumcision, who worship God in the Spirit, rejoice in Christ Jesus, and have **no confidence in the flesh.**"

He commands the believer: "*If then you were raised with Christ, seek those things which are above, where Christ is, sitting at the right hand of the God . . . for you died, and your life is hidden with Christ in God . . . Therefore put to death your members which are on the earth: fornication . . . but now you must also put off all these: anger . . . Therefore , as elect of God, holy and beloved, put on tender mercies, kindness, humbleness of mind, meekness and longsuffering*" (Colossians 3:1, 3, 5, 8, 12).

But the very heart of this pivotal verse (v.6) is: our old man was crucified with Him. The original scripture combines his death and ours as a veritable *co-crucifixion.* We were in him, we accompanied him in that death. We in our representative died when he died and were separated forever from the power and control of the sin nature. This reality is seminal in its consequences.

This truth must be believed and obeyed. Again this truth is a personal and practical knowing at the intimate level of heart and will. We are cast on the Holy Spirit to accomplish this in the breaking and humbling of the believer:

Isaiah combines the wonders of a sovereign God with lowliness of heart. "*For thus says the High and Lofty One who inhabits eternity, whose name is Holy: I dwell in the high and holy place, with him who has a contrite and humble spirit, and to revive the heart of the contrite ones*" (Isaiah 57:15). It is through our accepting in faith God's breaking, not our effort to believe, that the power of his death is released in us. There is no other way.

The key verse: Romans 6:6

"that the body of sin might be done away with"

The "body of sin" is all we inherit from the First Adam, our mortal body that becomes so easily the vehicle and agent of sin. The key verb is "katargeo"; to be idle, to render inactive, useless and ineffective . . . *to abrogate, make void, do away with, put an end to* [italics mine].[14]

Our identification with Christ in his death once for all to the power of sin (Romans 6:10) puts an end to the rule and control of sin as a principle. It does not leave a void or a vacuum because we are saved by his life (5: 10); his risen life is now our inheritance. We are now adopted sons of God with full authority to claim the inheritance in a victorious Christ.

We must exercise care in understanding the scope of this death, our death in him. The essence is to cancel the power and authority of the sin principle; in brief, to annul its impact. God put the sin nature in neutral. The engine in neutral may roar, but it goes nowhere.

Two cars after a head-on collision are no longer serviceable as transportation, but there is no doubt that they originally were cars. Our identification with Christ is God's judicial verdict about **the power of grace to reign** in the believer made new in Christ. God will have nothing more to do with the old nature.

Here some have overstated this vital truth in their sincere zeal for holiness, making it mean a "human experience" much sought after. There has been no eradication of the potential power of sin to impact Paul; he remembers too vividly an occasion when he was powerless to not covet. It was,

---

[14] Ibid. pp. 841,842.

however, an abnormality, not the pattern of the Christian life (Romans 7:7-24).

The key verse: Romans 6:6

"that we should no longer be slaves of sin"

The end result is liberation, freedom to not sin, holiness of life. Our enslavement to sin is turned into our enslavement to the one who died that we might live his life here and now: *"But God be thanked that though you were slaves of sin, yet you obeyed from the heart that form of doctrine to which you were delivered. And having been set free from sin, you became slaves of righteousness"* (Romans 6: 17, 18).

"I cannot believe in 'sinless perfection' in this life (1 John 1:6, 8, 10; 2:1-3), nor do I advocate sinful imperfection!" a quotation of L. E. Maxwell, as remembered] a willingness to tolerate and rationalize the rule of pride and bitterness.

All too often we are encouraged to try and be like Christ, to do our very best. Such attempts can only be led to abject frustration because *"the flesh profits nothing"* (John 6: 63).

A brief personal testimony for what it is worth

Those who know me know that Romans 6:6 has been my personal verse, the story of some 64 years of ministry. I was blessed to be raised in a godly home with an Irish mother who challenged us to holiness. I was highly privileged to graduate from Prairie Bible Institute high school (4 years--'46), Prairie Bible Institute (3 years--'49), another Bible college (2 years--'51). There have been many academic honors, but more importantly at 14 while in high school, I responded to the call of missions. I sought to be truly God's, but much in the power of the flesh, hence a deep "spiritual pride" that masked my troublesome sinful thoughts.

In my first small mission pastorate in Winnipeg at 21 years of age, I began a series of expositional studies on Romans to challenge my members to live a holy life. I had a sense of personal achievement because I knew so much! In the midst of preaching one winter Sunday morning on Romans 6:6, the Spirit said to me -- no voice -- "Gordon, you are a hypocrite! You know nothing of what you preach." A lightning bolt could not have destroyed me more effectively.

That night in a prayer of desperation I said: "Lord, let it cost me what it may cost me, I must know the truth of Romans 6:6. [I thought I knew it backward and forward doctrinally]. If you don't show me, I must resign from the ministry."

God heard that prayer of spiritual hunger but answered it, not at all, however, as I would have chosen. A few months later I received an invitation for the first time to be a conference speaker for five days in St. Vincent, Minnesota, a church where I was well-known. My first thought was: "Great, now they have discovered me!" But I knew I should not think that way, but those thoughts were indeed **my** thoughts! I quenched that thought, my thought. So I prepared diligently and went to speak, saying sincerely that I wanted to glorify God and edify his people.

Upon arriving on Saturday, I was informed that another brother, E. V. Folden, would share the days. The interim pastor asked me to preach Sunday morning. Again my proud thought: "I was chosen above my fellow pastor." Of course, I "humbly" accepted the invitation.

I spoke from my heart on *The Offering Up of Isaac* in Genesis 22. That passage had had a profound impact on my personal life. God had asked me pointedly to break the very serious relationship with my girlfriend, today my wife, as a proof of my exclusive love for Him. I obeyed him and like Abraham I received a great spiritual reward.

In the afternoon it was E. V. Folden's turn to speak, but he did not go up to the platform but simply stood below and opened his Bible. I had come with the thought of analyzing his message, but God had another message for me. I cannot remember anything E.V. Folden said.

God took a severe dealing with my "spiritual pride" and inner failures. I saw myself as never before - a darkened heart worthy of death. It was as if I saw myself, a hideous figure, there on the Cross.

Then came clearly to mind a word from God, his recalling my earlier prayer of desperation: **"Let it cost me what it may cost me, I must know . . . ."** **"I want you to tell these your friends just who you really are as I know you!!"** "But, Lord, they will send me home on the next bus." But I had earlier vowed: "Lord, if you speak, I will obey."

I don't remember if Brother Folden had finished his message or not, but I stood up and asked to speak. I did not go up to the platform as in the morning, I assure you. I spoke of my "spiritual pride" and the inner battles I had lost with evil thoughts. Then the fountains of my soul broke open. I stood and sobbed. I knew I could not speak another word, so I sat down.

To my amazement, Romans 6:6, my earlier text came immediately to mind, and I found myself repeating *"Knowing this, Gordon Johnson, was crucified…."* For the first time in my life I was free. I had no mask. I had no reputation.

The wonder that followed was that a true revival visited us, not because of my preaching but in part because of my humbling; the meeting was not dismissed until several hours later. Several began to confess their sins publicly.

When the meeting was finally dismissed, I wondered, now what? But to my surprise the pastor said: "I want you to preach tonight." Now my first inward response was: "But Lord, I can't. I'm not worthy." To which God seemed to say: "You never will be worthy to open my book, but preach."

I assure you I made no mental comparison now with my speaker friend. I preached a different message: the anointing of the High Priest; first the blood applied to the right ear, finger and foot and then the anointing oil of the Spirit (Leviticus 8).

That Sunday evening I called my wife, Grace, in Winnipeg; her response was immediate: "what has happened to you?" I was a different husband in process. That night I couldn't fall asleep for joy because of the new sense of spiritual relief. But I finally fell asleep but was awakened after midnight by the sound of car arriving and noises below in the home of my host.

The next morning at breakfast my hostess said: "Last night the Kochendoffers--a well-known family in the church--came by to make things right between us" [They were the two most prominent families]. They came in their coats covering their night attire in the dead of winter in the middle of the night and the two couples were reconciled before the Lord. While they were on civil speaking terms, it was evident that jealousy and pride had been at the root of their rivalry.

Then my hostess said something that really shook me with reference to my testimony: "I didn't know that you preachers had hearts just like we do." What an indictment on our ministerial pride!

Five days of revival continued with reconciliations and a spiritual breakthrough in a good church that proved to have more divisions than anyone could have thought.

God had to break me publicly. I now knew what happened to Gordon Johnson at the cross. I saw myself there, deserving what was mine, death. I now could take to heart what was his, his risen life. I would like to be able to say that such a public humiliation was the final blow to my pride. By no means. But now I knew how to take my stand at the Cross.

Every time I do it, there is the release in the Spirit. Whenever I choose to not reckon myself dead to sin, the flesh rules. There have been ups and downs, shame for inner thoughts. But now that I stand under that verdict of death to self, I can enjoy his risen life, Christ's life.

Conclusion

Such a public humiliation may not be God's way to bring you to know your death with Christ, but in some way there must be a breaking, an unlearning of our selfish independence. God is the master artist who brings to us: circumstances, allowing our failures to remind us of our selfishness, our sinfulness: a sickness, a calamity, maybe an unjust treatment, anything that reduces us by that painful unlearning process that leads to life eternal. *"For the kingdom of God is not food and drink, but righteousness, and peace and joy in the Holy Spirit"* (Romans 14:17).

A life of overcoming, a life of ceaseless praise,
Be this thy blessed portion throughout the coming days.

The victory was purchased on Calvary's cross for thee,
Sin shall not have dominion, the Son hath made you free.

And would'st know the secret of constant victory?
Let in the Overcomer, and he will conquer thee!
Thy broken spirit, taken In sweet captivity
Shall glory in His triumph and share His victory.

Then from thy life ascending one triumph note of praise,
(For they who always conquer a victor's song must raise),
Shall echo on unceasing till Satan's hosts doth flee
Before our glorious watchword, "Lord, victory for me."

Though all the path before thee the host of darkness fill,
Look to thy Father's promise, and claim the victory still.
Faith sees the heavenly legions, where doubt sees nought
but foes,
And through the very conflict her life the stronger grows.

More stern will grow the conflict as near our King's return,
And they alone can face it who this great lesson learn:-
That from them God asks nothing but to unlatch the door
Admitting Him, who through them will conquer evermore.

--Freda Hanbury Allen

Chapter 15: The key verse-the process of "knowing this"

Chapter 16

PRACTICAL STEPS OF FAITH AND OBEDIENCE

Romans 6: 7-14

Now Paul can delve more deeply into the heart of the doctrine of sanctification or Christ-likeness. The truth was begun in Romans 5:12. We were born into the First Adam, **born in sin** and the effects of that nature we continue to carry. However, we were born anew in the Last Adam-- we **died to sin.** The effects of that new nature now reign in the believer by grace through faith.

While tensions between the two remain a factor, the reality of being in Christ, united to him in death to sin and raised to walk in his risen life is a **MUCH MORE** relationship (Romans 5:9, 10, 15, 17, 20).

The question can now be answered categorically: Shall we keep on sinning (6:1)? Perish that thought! We died to sin in respect to its control and power over us. From that judicial death in our representative, we share his death, burial and resurrection.

That profound union must be progressively known at a heart and experience level (Romans 6:6), the work of the Holy Spirit making it real in our co crucifixion with him. This is a walk of faith and gratitude for what he did at the Cross once and for all in us. *"Knowing this that our old man was co crucified with Him, that the body of sin might be done away with* [that is, rendered impotent, its power cancelled] *that we should not serve sin."*

The Severing Power of Death, the Ground of This New Union
Romans 6:7-10

Paul in these verses rings the changes on the effect of death in the legal realm; death ends the bonds and power of any previous relationship. In the spiritual realm we are now married to another (Romans 7:4-6) and live in freedom from the condemnation of the law by the Holy Spirit who lives in us; all of this newness comes to us in grace through faith in Christ's vicarious death (Romans 8:1-4).

Paul appeals to the inability of the law to extract any further judgment on a dead man. When Hitler died in the Berlin bunker in 1945, no world court could further punish him: his infamy would live on but no human power could touch him. The text says death ends the legal process: death clears the guilty of further retribution. The offender has paid the ultimate price, his own life.

This truth was emphasized greatly when on a walking tour in Edinburgh, Scotland, in 1977, we came on a plaque in a public square where in years past they had publicly hung the criminal. The following day a notice of death would read: So and So was justified yesterday at such and such an hour. The poor criminal had indeed been justified, but unfortunately he was also dead, dead. Not so with our justification. We died but we live again in a new vital relationship with a risen Christ.

Since it has been established that we died with Christ (v.2), we have been cleared of any further retribution by the law. With good reason Paul states: *"For he who has died has been freed from sin"* (v.7). It follows ipso facto that we will live with

Chapter 16: Practical steps of faith and obedience"

him: his death and resurrection are uniquely bound together. Since we share one, we share the other (v. 8).

Paul expounds on the consequences of our identification in that death and resurrection. Our position is final, definitive. His death was a cosmic and fatal blow to the principle of sin in union with the First Adam; Christ now lives in us.

Paul has now arrived at the important juncture and is about to apply the truth of his death and, in reality our death, to the walk of faith. Follow his reasoning: *"Now if"*—since—*"we died with Christ"*--a sure established fact—*"we believe that we shall also live with Him, knowing that Christ, having been raised from the dead, dies no more. Death no longer has dominion over him"* (vv.8, 9).

In this verse Paul uses a different Greek verb, we "believe" or we "know" that speaks to an historical fact. His death and its vicarious value are an uncontroverted historical fact. No one will ever question that he cannot die again. His death was final and ultimate. His final words: "**It is finished**" (John 19:30).

Now comes the deepest value of that death to the believer. *"For the death that He died, He **died to sin** once for all; but the life that He lives, He lives unto God"* (v.10). Once again no one would ever question the reality of His once for all death and his return to live unto his Father.

But before Paul makes the practical application to our walk of faith (v.11), we must observe that the text specifically says that Christ **died to sin**: this is precisely the exact grammatical structure or phrase that is applied to **our death to sin** in union with him (v.2). This is no coincidence; it speaks to the absolute equality of the value of his death to destroy or annul the power of sin in the believer (v.6).

Chapter 16: Practical steps of faith and obedience"

The Role of Faith and Obedience in This Union
Romans 6:11-13

We come now to the believer's response. Until this moment, Paul has highlighted almost exclusively what Christ did for us and in us at the cross (Romans 6:1-10). We will observe that *the action verbs are in the passive voice in the past tense.* This is what he did once and for all in our behalf. Until now there are no action verbs in the indicative or imperative mood, no commands that call for our response. **But now everything changes.**

There is a series of four commands addressed directly to the believer. Three of these verbs are in the imperative mood, present tense *reckon or count on* (v.11), *do not let sin* reign (v.12), *do not present* (v.13a) and one in the imperative with an aspect of decisive, definitive action in the immediate aorist present *but present yourselves* (v.13 b).The present tense in the original Greek carries an ongoing action to be understood.

1. *Be Counting Yourselves Dead to Sin and Alive to God*
Romans 6:11

It is a tragedy that these four commands are not first and foremost in every treatment of victory over sin. Have you ever heard a sermon preached on these verses? We almost never hear a clear and emphatic explanation of these verses. For a course in counseling that I taught, I searched to see if in any these verses were included in preparation for the counselor. To my amazement I found only one textbook with a reference to these critical verses. The rest had good psychological advice, but our problem needs more than good advice.

Yet these verses, steps of faith and obedience, are the open doorway to victory. On occasion we may hear of four secrets or ten steps to victory. More confusion reigns and victory eludes our best efforts. Paul in Romans six gives us the simplest and clearest commands grounded in what Christ did for us once and for all on the Cross, the simplicity of faith.

Until now in Romans 6 we have not been asked to do anything whatsoever. What has been done, God in Christ did. Now, however, there will be only **one inclusive command: reckon, count on, present, believe and implicit in faith is obedience.** We are called upon to choose in faith. More than that, we cannot ever do anything else. Once the crowd asked Jesus: *"'What shall we do, that we may work the works of God.' Jesus answered and said to them, 'This is the work of God, that **you believe in Him whom He sent'"** (John 6:28, 29).

Before examining the first command of faith, there is a question to be asked. When you trusted Christ as your Savior, what did you contribute? What did you do to earn your salvation? The answer is simple indeed: absolutely nothing; you accepted in faith the free gift of eternal life.

Repentance was implicit but it was the simplicity of trust and you received God's gift. In fact, Paul in writing to the Colossians sums up the Christian life in its entirety: *"As you have therefore received Christ Jesus the Lord, so walk in Him"* (Colossians 2:6). All too often we have turned the Christian life upside down into our works righteousness. How sad and too often true!

Note carefully that this key verse begins with *"**likewise.**"* Don't take this adverb for granted. In the very **same manner as he died to sin, you must count on, reckon on your death to sin.** If his death to sin is sufficient, then yours follows invariably, inexorably. You can add nothing to **his death to sin** nor can you add to **your death to sin.** There is no penance, no delay, no tarrying, no fasting. It is an accomplished fact. It is yours to accept, to count on.

The verb "reckon" is really an accounting term and was used in the purchase of grain and common merchandise. The money is there and you exercise the use of it for your desired end. This is not a question of feelings, emotions, or experiences; it is grounded in divine reality as God sees it. Victory is ours in trusting, resting in his work and in his integrity.

The exercise of simple faith is really a two barreled acceptance. The text clearly requires both expressions of faith. We count equally on our death to the old life as we count on our new life in Christ. The Christian life is a balance of the negative that opens up the positive. He died and rose again, a single death/resurrection fact. The Christian life is a balanced rejection of the old and a positive acceptance of the new relationship established by God himself. Once again it has been his work and we count on its completeness.

We often hear in a general way that the Spirit will do his work and indeed he does. But we seem seldom to see his work wrought out in our lives and the lives of those around us. Can we blame the Holy Spirit for his not working? Has he been unfaithful in his own ministry? Of course not!

If we don't see the Spirit doing his work in our midst, the answer is self-evident. We have been walking in the flesh; he can have nothing to do with your flesh and mine.

The Holy Spirit does his work wherever the Cross does its death dealing and life giving work by faith; the Spirit is there in absolute faithfulness to do what only he can do. But he works in union with the Cross that cancels out the flesh and frees him to introduce the life of a risen Christ. Paul has balance in saying: put off, make to die, put off, put on (Colossians 4:5, 8, 12).

Have you noticed that there is no overt mention of the Spirit in Romans 6? The reason is that Paul must establish first the truth of our union with Christ, as the ground of his later work to be introduced in Romans 7:1-6. He is after all the Spirit of Truth (John 14:17). First, truth believed and received and accepted gratefully, then his quickening work of grace in response to faith.

Again Paul returns to use the imperative mood, a command, but it is not a once for all faith/obedience but rather a constant ongoing counting on our death and our resurrection. Our act of faith becomes an act and an attitude of faith and acceptance.

2. Don't Be Letting Sin Reign in Your Mortal Body Romans 6:12

A second command follows logically. Paul denies the reign of sin as a principle, but he admits sin's presence by stating in "*your mortal body*." He recognizes the reality of the presence of sin but will not yield to the reign of sin in the believer. When Christ gives to us our transformed body, then in his presence the presence of sin will be abolished.

Implicit in this second command: ***don't let sin be reigning*** is the clear inference that there is absolutely no need for sin to ever reign, granted God's ongoing work of grace. There must be something inherent in the first command that frees the believer from the demand to sin. Said positively the believer does not have to sin. He may sin in the measure in which he does not believe and grasp the practical breaking ministry of the Holy Spirit.

I repeat again that there is no mention of the Holy Spirit's work in Romans 6. However, the truth of our identification with Christ at the Cross must first be believed and gratefully received, then, and only then, can the Spirit of Truth do his work.

3. Don't Be Presenting Your Members as Ammunition to the Sin Principle   Romans 6:13a

Once again, "present" is the same imperative mood and ongoing present tense as it is characteristically in Greek. Stop the habit of your members: mind, eyes, hands, emotions, etc., being slaves or victims of the sin principle. This is an active personal OBEDIENCE. True Biblical faith devolves invariably into obedience. A faith that does not involve obedience is a dead faith, as James makes so clear. Faith and obedience are forever wed together.

Here is a clarion call to follow through with obedient faith. Once again the response is to count, stop the inertia of sin by presenting our members. The verb "present"' is crucial to Romans 6 and 12, but the two usages are usually disconnected. The challenge to present our bodies as living sacrifices (Romans 12:1, 2) without having presented our members and our wills to the risen Lord is a nonstarter.

The verb "present" is actually a military term or a term used in bringing sacrifices. It is never a work of merit but rather an attitude of absolute willingness to respond to the command of what is to come. The soldier presents himself to his colonel with no knowledge of what may be required. But his is an attitude of readiness and willingness to obey unconditionally. There must be a pattern, a habit of presenting the members as instruments or armament for righteousness.

Chapter 16: Practical steps of faith and obedience"

4. Be Presenting Now and Decisively the Essence of Your Will   Romans 6:13b

The change in the verb tense is not seen in English, but it reflects the aorist in Greek that speaks to the aspect of the quality of action, decisive, final and irrevocable. It signifies a heart commitment at a deeper level. The believer has counted on that identification in death and resurrection; he has stopped the inertia of letting sin reign; he has stopped presenting his members as willing subjects of the old and has made that heart commitment.

This is the pattern. This is the road map that will lead to victory. If there is failure along the way, and there may and probably will be, the believer returns to confess his sin (I John 1:9) and takes the cleansing of the blood and returns to his standing and position in a risen Christ: the blood for cleansing and the Cross for victory.

Sin Shall Not Have Dominion Over You   Romans 6:14

The four steps outlined above are undergirded by the simple fact that *we are not under law but under grace.* Victory is a grace work from beginning to end. Our only response is to reckon, count on what Christ did 2000 years ago and now to let simple faith activate the reality of a victory that God purchased in the name of his Son. We share in that life and share in that victory.

Please notice the fine balance of the four commands. The first and the last, reckon and present yourselves are positive commands within the reach of faith. The second and third are negative commands: stop letting sin reign and stop presenting your members.

Chapter 16: Practical steps of faith and obedience"

Conclusion

The key concept of the Message of the Cross is faith in our union with Christ crucified and risen again. Faith issues in obedience to him. Another key concept is the verb PRESENT: (6:13 twice; 12:1). The essence of the verb is not action or struggle, nor merit but availability, place yourself at his command, even a military term—readiness, unquestioned obedience, not doing but being open and receptive to what God did and wants to do through the Spirit of Truth.

Paul will virtually sum up the whole of this magnificent epistle with one note of praise. "*Now may the God of hope fill you with all joy and peace in BELIEVING, that you may abound in hope by the power of the Holy Spirit*" (Romans 15:13). The Christian walk is a walk of faith of gratefully believing.

These truths free us for the struggle to maintain what God has given. **Our responsibility is faith and obedience and everything else is subsumed under that.** Notice the absence of reference in Paul's road to victory of reading the Bible, prayer and other disciplines that follow. These four steps are laid hold of as the dynamic; then the disciplines that the Christ life brings will follow in the maintenance of our spiritual life. As we were saved, so we walk. "*As you have therefore received Christ Jesus the Lord, so walk in Him*" (Colossians 2: 6).

Buried with Christ, and raised with Him too; what is there left for me to do?
Simply to cease from struggling and strife, simply to walk in newness of life.
Glory be to God.

Chapter 16: Practical steps of faith and obedience"

Risen with Christ, my glorious Head; holiness now the pathway I tread,
Beautiful thought, while walking therein: he that is dead is freed from sin.
Glory be to God.

Living with Christ, who dieth no more, following Christ who goeth before;
I am from bondage utterly freed, reckoning self as dead indeed.
Glory be to God.

Living for Christ, my members I yield, servants to God, for evermore sealed,
Not under law, I'm under grace, sin is dethroned and Christ takes its place.
Glory be to God.

Growing in Christ; no more shall be named things of which now I'm truly ashamed,
Fruit unto holiness will I bear; life evermore, the end I shall share.
Glory be to God.

--T. Ryder

Chapter 17

THE REIGNING LIFE IN CHRIST NOW IN ACTION

Romans 6:15-23

After beginning with the penetrating question: *"Shall we continue in sin that grace may abound?"* (Romans 6:1), Paul answers it categorically. By no means, because **we *died to sin,*** *"how shall we who **died to sin** live any longer in it"* (6:2)?

This seems such a radical remedy for our age-old sin problem. But in my favorite verse, Romans 6:6, Paul says*: **"knowing this that our old man was co crucified with Him . . . ."*** It is tragic that this basic truth is so seldom referred to in preaching or in hymnody. We were **BORN CRUCIFIED** as the French theologian Lacordaire wisely said. This is also the eye-catching title of my mentor, Rev. L.E. Maxwell's first and now classic book on union with Christ. I personally owe so much to his example and teaching.

That glorious fact liberates us from sin's power; now the walk of faith is before us as our new perspective and point of departure. Paul then lays out for us the steps of *knowing*, the very essence of how we must daily walk in the light of these basic truths.

Paul sets forth those truths in Romans 6: 11-14. Four choices are before the believing saint.

1. *Be counting yourself dead to sin and alive to God* (6:11) a heart FAITH, a positive action and attitude.
2. *Don't be letting sin reign in your mortal body* (6:12) a resolute negative response of the renewed will to any continued sinning.
3. *Don't be presenting your members as ammunition to the sin principle* (6:13a), a further negative response of the renewed will.
4. *Present yourself decisively now* (6:13b) — a heart OBEDIENCE of availability to the risen life of Christ.

Take note of the more literal translations of the Greek text. The translation may sound awkward but the emphasis falls squarely on the ongoing progressive nature of our faith and obedience. This is borne out by the *knowing this*, of Romans 6:6, a gerund that involves incessant action and vigilance. Little wonder that Christ so often warned his disciples to watch and pray (Matthew 26:41; Luke 21:36). The walk of faith is a vigilance, an act that become an ongoing daily attitude.

Between the first and second command there has evidently been a profound enablement. It is not in the power of our will to reject sin's dynamic but rather the dynamic of the Cross, the crossing out of our best efforts enabling us to take a stand against our sin nature. There is spiritual power in that death, our death. It was God who severed the relationship and we only assent to it in simple faith

In the second command and in the third command by inference, Paul stresses the verb to "reign." There is the assumption that the sin principle does remain, but it has no legitimate right to reign. On the contrary, the believer is free to present actively his members as instruments of righteousness to God.

Finally, in the fourth command the Greek aorist tense, whose meaning is lost to us in English, stresses not only the past aspect but the finality or quality of the action is decisively over. The earlier tenses were present progressive implying ongoing action. But the Cross terminated our relationship to the sin principle.

Sin shall not have dominion over you (v.14)--the ongoing result of the walk of FAITH and OBEDIENCE. God promises the believer liberty, freedom from sin's power. We are now under grace, no longer under the law that condemns us.

The True Marks of Holiness-Character and Conduct Romans 6:15-18

Theory and practice may often appear to be two very different things; Paul faces our dilemma head on with an echo of the same question (cf., 6:1):*"What then? Shall we sin because we are not under law but under grace?"* (6:15). He gives the same resounding answer: *"Certainly not."*

Paul's answer is self-evident. *"Do you not know that to whom you present yourselves slaves to obey, you are that one's slave whom you obey, whether of sin to death, or of obedience to righteousness"* (v.16). "He who drags his chain is not free," no matter how loudly he claims freedom. Paul in essence is saying it is a simple question of **to whom you present yourselves.** He is building on the new point of departure. A faith that trusts and chooses righteousness will resolve the issue of what the believer's walk will look like.

True faith is not "belief", so often defined as head knowledge, but truth believed and obeyed, *"obedience from* the heart to which you were delivered." Here is the fundamental transaction that does not allow for mere imitation of Christ but rather heart participation in the risen life of Christ. We have transferred our slavery from sin now to become willing slaves to righteousness in our Savior. What a blessed transfer!

In the verse that follows (v.17), Paul bursts forth with a decisive word of thanksgiving. You were slaves to sin, but now you obeyed from the heart a new pattern or mold of living into which you were poured. The image is a mold and the resulting shape the clay must take. Dr. Huegel, my mentor and longtime missionary in Mexico (1920-1970), often said: *"Praise is faith in full bloom."* Why not let faith break forth in thanksgiving! To believe is to receive both in initial salvation and in sanctification.

In presenting ourselves--our renewed will--to him, we choose to be slaves to righteousness, a new master that lifts our burdens and lightens our heart. This reality is reflected beautifully in Exodus 21: 1-6. Slavery could never be the future of a son of Abraham. After serving six years as a slave, he could go out free. But if he chose to stay with his master and his family and said plainly: *"I love my master, my wife and my children, I will not go out free, then his master shall bring him to the judges. He shall also bring him to the door, or to a doorpost, and his master shall pierce his ear with an awl; and he shall serve him forever."* The former slave is free to love his master and his family in that order. He has no more ear for the siren sounds of self, the world and the devil. What a new focus! What a new blessed freedom!

A Sad Past Parallel that Operates as a Guide in the New Sphere of Life   Romans 6:19-22

Paul draws a remarkably clear parallel between what we used to be as slaves of sin prior to knowing Christ and our new living relationship in Christ. We presented our members as slaves to uncleanness and lawlessness leading to more lawlessness. But now comes a paradigmatic change, a change not of degree but of kind. *"So now **present** your members as slaves of righteousness for holiness"* (v.19). You hear the echo of: *"**Present** yourselves to God as being alive from the dead and your members as instruments of righteousness to God"* *(v.13).*

That word **"present"** is key to the process. Its essential meaning is to make oneself available, to place oneself under the orders of another, a military term. It is not our doing, nor our service rendered but our openness to God's Holy Spirit by obeying the truth. What is a new act of faith becomes a constant attitude of believing and gratefully obeying.

Paul will deal with the role of the Spirit shortly. But truth obeyed inevitably brings the active dynamic of the Holy Spirit. Holiness is not our doing; it was his doing at the Cross and our embracing it by faith and obedience. If holiness were our doing, it would foster our pride of grace; it would be the most reprehensive thing with which we could insult our God! It would, in effect, say your Son died in vain! (Galatians 2: 21).

Paul reminds us of the fruitlessness and deception of our former life. But by an amazing contrast just the opposite is now ours. *"But now having been set free from sin, and having become slaves of God, you have your fruit unto holiness, and the end, everlasting life"* (v.22). As you well know, everlasting life is not only quantity and duration, but foremost it is the actual quality of the divine life of God himself to be embraced here and now.

God's Final Summation   Romans 6:23

"For the wages of sin is death, but the gift of God is eternal life in Christ Jesus our Lord." How often this verse is quoted out of its proper context! Whenever quoted, however, it is a divine reality. That is taken for granted, but the context determines its application. God is stating to his children as a categorical reality. There are only two roads, two destinies, totally incompatible one to the other. It is either a life of sin under its domination or a life of holiness in union with Christ Jesus. There is no question but there is only one way open to the believer in Christ.

God states his opposition to any compromise or concession to sin as a principle. He has saved us from it. He has made a full provision for our life of victory. But much more is involved. That life of victory is a gift of God, not a reward to be gained or maintained by our doing. True life is Christ, a gracious gift to be received and embraced. *"Christ in you, the hope of glory"* (Colossians 1:27).

Often we miss the beauty of Christ in us by overlooking the simplicity of our coming to him in our need and finding in him the fulfillment of our deepest heart's desire. Our Lord on several occasions graciously invited those with need. *"On the last day, that great day of the feast, Jesus stood and cried out, saying, 'If anyone thirsts, let him come to Me and drink. He who believes in Me, as the Scripture has said, "Out of his heart will flow rivers of living water"'"* (John 7:37, 38).

Matthew reminds us of the same invitation: *"Come to Me, all you who labor and are heavy laden, and I will give you rest.*

*Take My yoke upon you and learn from Me, for I am gentle and lowly in heart, and **you will find rest for your souls**, for My yoke is easy and My burden is light"* (Matthew 11:28-30).

Sometimes hymnody expresses the free gift of grace better than prose.

> Out of my bondage, sorrow and night,
> Jesus! I come, Jesus, I come!
> Into Thy freedom, gladness and light,
> Jesus, I come to Thee!
> Out of my sickness into Thy health,
> Out of my want and into Thy wealth,
> Out of my sin and into Thyself,
> Jesus, I come to Thee.
>
> Out of my shameful failure and loss,
> Jesus! I come, Jesus, I come!
> Into the glorious gain of Thy cross,
> Jesus, I come to Thee!
> Out of earth's sorrows into Thy balm,
> Out of life's storms and into Thy calm,
> Out of distress to jubilant psalm,
> Jesus, I come to Thee!
>
> Out of unrest and arrogant pride,
> Jesus, I come! Jesus, I come!
> Into Thy blessed will to abide,
> Jesus, I come to Thee!
> Out of myself to dwell in Thy love,
> Out of despair into raptures above,
> Upward for aye on wings like a dove,

Jesus, I come to Thee!

Out of the fear and dread of the tomb,
Jesus, I come! Jesus, I come!
Into the joy and light of thy home,
Jesus, I come to Thee!
Out of the depths of ruin untold,
Into the peace of Thy sheltering fold,
Ever Thy glorious face to behold,
Jesus, I come to Thee!

--William T. Sleeper

Paul still has further practical truths to face as in Romans 7. First, he shares the reality of our spiritual marriage to the resurrected Christ allowing the Holy Spirit to introduce a new paradigm: *"that we should serve in the newness of his Spirit and not in the oldness of the letter"* (v.6)

Then to our surprise but not a surprise to our experience, he remembers an occasion when he lived a time of deep personal failure, even as a called apostle. But then when he returned to his position in Christ, united in his death and resurrection, a life of victory, the joys of the Spirit-filled life are recorded for us in Romans 8.

But we must never lose sight of the reality of God's salvation being always and only a **gift of God**. *"For by grace you have been saved through faith, and that not of yourselves; it is the **gift of God,** not of works, lest anyone should boast. For we are His workmanship, created in Christ Jesus for good works, which God prepared beforehand that we should walk in them"* (Ephesians 2:8-10).

Practical Points to Ponder

1. God chose to put the "old life" to death, a cosmic, fatal blow to the sin principle (Romans 6:2; Colossians 3:3). There is now a new master, a new Lord.

2. The believer realizes this truth through the process of "knowing" (Romans 6:6), a God-illuminating act and attitude of faith and obedience.

3. The risen life in the believer is God's gracious gift and will always be his work of grace through faith, not our efforts and struggle.

Chapter 18

THE BELIEVER MARRIED TO ANOTHER – THE RISEN CHRIST

Romans 7:1-6

Until now in Paul's treatment of sanctification or personal holiness, he has laid out for us the truth of our position in Christ. His treatment has been thorough and basic.

But additional truths are now provided for our personal walk. In our Lord's Upper Room Discourse, he shared four times with his disciples the coming of the Holy Spirit as the "other" Comforter, the other Advocate (John 14:17; 15:26; 16:7). It is interesting to note that the word "other" means an advocate of the identical essence and function.

*"Nevertheless I tell you the truth. It is to your **advantage** that I go away; for if I do not go away, the Helper will not come to you; but if I depart, I will send Him to you . . . However, when He, the Spirit of Truth, has come, He will guide you into all truth; He will not speak on His own authority, but whatever He hears He will speak; and He will tell you things to come. He will glorify Me, for He will take of what is Mine and declare it to you"* (John 16: 7, 13, 14).

Until now in the epistle of Romans God through Paul has laid out for us the **TRUTH** of our union with Christ in his death and resurrection. Christ had plainly said:" *If you abide in My word, you are My disciples indeed. And you shall know the truth, and*

Chapter 18: The believer married to another-the risen Christ

146

the truth shall make you free" (John 8:31, 32). *"It is the Spirit who gives life; the flesh profits nothing. The words that I speak to you are spirit, and they are life"* (John 6:63).

This is a most important truth to lay hold of. The Holy Spirit, the new personal dynamic of the victorious life in Christ, is, after all, the Spirit of Truth promised by Jesus. Paul also calls him the Spirit of Christ. *"Now if anyone does not have the Spirit of Christ, he is not His"* (Romans 8:9).

The Role of Truth, Grace and the Holy Spirit--A Divine Triad

The key to the fullness of the Christ life in the believer is the balance and the unity of these truths.

First, we grasp by faith the liberating **truths** of what God did at the Cross, forgiving our sins, ***Christ for us.*** *"And you, being dead in your trespasses and the uncircumcision of your flesh, He has made alive together with Him, having forgiven you all trespasses"* (Colossians 2:13). In addition to the forgiveness of all sins past, present and future in a guaranteed eternal position, he has judged once and for all the flesh. *"Knowing this, that our old man was co-crucified with Him, that the body of sin might be done away with, that we should no longer serve sin"* (Romans 6:6).

These are the foundational truths of the believer in Christ. We so seldom hear of the Christian life being in its essence **our death to sin** (Romans 6:2) as was **his *death to sin*** (Romans 6:10).

Second, we grasp by faith the deeper understanding that all that God did for us and in us in Christ was in the fullness of his grace. ***Grace,*** an aspect of God's infinite love, was the original motivation and the dynamic that carried out God's eternal plan. There surely could be no merit or value in the rebellious sinner. Salvation could only come from the heart of an infinitely gracious God.

The classic statement of Paul says it all: *"For by grace you have been saved through faith, and that not of yourselves; it is the gift of God, not of works, lest anyone should boast. For we are God's workmanship [poem] created in Christ Jesus for good works prepared beforehand that we should walk in them"* (Ephesians 2: 8-10).To magnify his work of grace he has *"raised us up and seated us in heavenly places in Christ Jesus, that in the ages to come He might show the exceeding riches of His grace in His kindness toward us in Christ Jesus"* (Ephesians 2:6, 7).

His **grace** eliminates our striving, our doing. It has been forever his doing once and for all. It is ours in the hymn writer's classic verse, "to trust and obey for there is no other way to be happy in Jesus, but to trust and obey."

Third, the **Holy Spirit** is now about to be presented as the modus operandi of the Christian life. He is the executor of the truth and grace who will do his liberating work in us. He will do it faithfully and on his terms of time and place. In brief, this is what it means to grow in grace or spiritual maturity. The Christian life is an act of faith that becomes an attitude of faith and an ongoing process. *"The just shall live by faith"* (Rom. 1:17).

Paul Reviews for Us the Work of Grace at the Cross

Notice carefully Paul's review of TRUTH. He is about to illustrate our new point of departure to live the Christian life, that is, our death to sin accomplished once for all (Romans 6:2, 6). As that truth unfolds, we are to reckon or count ourselves dead indeed to sin and alive to God (v.11), not letting sin reign (v.12) nor continuing to present our members by default to the old way of life (v.12 a) but rather a decisive presenting of our heart and will to God (v.13b).

Now comes the affirmation of the new spiritual reality: *"For sin shall not have dominion over you, for you are not under law but under grace"* (v.14). Here is the TRUTH of the cross and the fact of GRACE being God's modus operandi (mode of working).

The Role of the Law is Now to be Considered

Paul is ready to introduce the next major step in the fullness of our salvation. Notice the parallel with Romans 6: 1, 3; first, the question is: *What shall we say then?* He follows up with his standard formula of surprise that such a basic truth should not be grasped: *"Or do you not know that as many of us were baptized into Christ Jesus Christ were baptized into his death?*

The parallel continues in 6:15: *What shall we say then?* After a brief summary of results 6:15-23 a second question follows in 7:1: *"Or do you not know, brethren (for I speak to those who know law), that the law has dominion over a man as long as he lives?"*

Paul bases his argument on what everyone takes for granted that there is an absolute break in any marriage interrupted by the death of a spouse. The widow is free to marry again, but only in the Lord. Before such a death she would be an adulteress, but after death she is now fit to enter another intimate relationship. What altered her status before the law? Simply the fact of the death of her spouse.

Grace in Action: We Are Free to Be Married to the Ascended Lord   Romans 7:4

If we can call Romans 6:6 The Magna Carta of our *identification* with Christ, then Romans 7: 4, 6 is the second Magna Carta of our *participation* in his risen life. (The Magna Carta was signed by King John of England in 1215 establishing the political basis for the nobles of that day to share in a limited way with the monarch, the genesis of our democratic political freedom).

Hear our Magna Carta: *"Therefore, my brethren, you also have become dead to the law through the body of Christ, that you may be married to another, even to Him who was raised from the dead, that we should bear fruit to God"* (v. 4). Here is a divine fact to be grasped by faith which begins a totally new dimension of our relationship; it is a spiritual marriage, our sharing in his risen life grounded in grace and the work of the cross.

This basic concept was introduced early in Romans 5:10: *"For if when we were enemies we were reconciled to God through the death of His son, **much more**, having been reconciled, we shall be saved by His life."* This is the "lost chord" of evangelical preaching, as Dr. F. J. Huegel (my mentor 1957-68) was accustomed to say.

The law, a transcript of God's moral perfection, rightly demanded perfection; we could never attain to it in the strength of our best endeavor. The old life persists and may still rule on occasion in areas of the believer's life, as Paul will illustrate shortly in his own sad personal experience (Romans 7:7-25).

But we are not shut up to that endless burden of struggle and striving. *"We are not under law but under grace"* (6:14).

But we must remember that truth was stated so clearly in 6:14 which in turn is followed by the paragraph (6:15-23) that reminds us that grace can never excuse sin nor be a partner with sin. On the contrary, *"But God be thanked that though you were slaves to sin, yet you obeyed from the heart that form of doctrine to which you were delivered. And having been set free from sin, you became* [past tense] *slaves to righteousness"* (Romans 6:17, 18).

In Paul's marriage analogy the woman [we] died "through the body of Christ" when he died. It follows that when he arose, the woman [we] arose now to be married to him who "was raised from the dead". Ours is now a relationship of love and not of duty to the law.

A whole new world of love and freedom becomes ours. ***This is a total transformation of the Christian life. The Christian life is not a duty, a debt and a demand but rather a love relationship to be honored and deepened, not by doing and duty but by being and sharing his risen life.***

The richness of this love relationship is yet to be followed up with the truths of the Holy Spirit and the reality of the old life still in us. We need to wait to see the whole picture as Paul unfolds it for us in the rest of chapter 7 and culminating in chapter 8.

The richness and depth of the Christian life are seen in the interaction between Truth, Grace and the Holy Spirit. Paul needs the full scope of Romans 5:12 to 8:39 (97 verses in all) to cover the wonders of the work of the Cross. Rapid deductions should not be made until we see the whole picture of victory now in a Risen Christ.

Marvelous grace of our loving Lord, grace that exceeds our sin and our guilt,
Yonder on Calvary's mount outpoured, there where the blood of the Lamb was spilt.

Chorus
Grace, grace, God's grace, grace that will pardon and cleanse within;
Grace, grace, God's grace, grace that is greater than all our sin.

Sin and despair like the sea waves cold, threaten the soul with infinite loss;
Grace that is greater, yes, grace untold, points to the Refuge, the mighty Cross.

Dark is the stain that we cannot hide, what can avail to wash it away?
Look! There is flowing a crimson tide; whiter than snow you may be today.

Marvelous, infinite matchless grace, freely bestowed on all who believe;
You that are longing to see His face, will you this moment His grace receive?

Julia H. Johnston

Chapter 19

LAW AND GRACE IN THE WALK OF FAITH

Romans 7

Paul has greatly enlarged our concept of the Christian life in Romans 7:1-6. He illustrates the reality of the death of either spouse that severs the bond of any legal marriage; now our death in union with Christ makes possible our being married to a risen Christ. We died to the law in the person of our Substitute (Romans 7:4). *"For I through the law died to the law that I might live to God. I have been crucified with Christ; it is no longer I who live, but Christ lives in me; and the life which I now live in the flesh I live by faith in the Son of God, who loved me and gave himself for me"* (Galatians 2:19, 20).

The **grace** of God, the **truth** of the Cross and now the **person** of the Holy Spirit, bring to fruition a love relationship. A whole new dimension has been added that transforms our daily walk from duty to delight. Christ becomes our life and living hope.

The thrust of the law was to condemn sin. *"Therefore by the deeds of the law no flesh will be justified in His sight, for by the law is the knowledge of sin"* (Romans 3:20). Paul adds, *"Cursed is everyone who does not continue in all thing which are written in the book of the law, to do them"* (Galatians 3:10).The law is a cruel taskmaster indeed, because the law demands absolute holiness and humility. Neither sinner nor saint in the strength of his best endeavor can ever match the law's demand.

Romans 7 speaks of our spiritual marriage to a risen Christ, a love relationship. All too often the Christian walk is portrayed as a struggle, a duty and our best effort to be like Christ. Instead of a duty to perform, Christ becomes our delight; resources are now available in that spiritual union with a Risen Savior, *"even to Him who was raised from the dead, that we should bear fruit unto God."*

Dr. Huegel liked to make the following comparison. Can you imagine a pretender showering his bride to be with flowers, chocolates and eloquent words of tender love and affection? But the morning after marital bliss, the bride finds a written set of rules which she is now committed to keep: "I must have my favorite breakfast at 7.00 sharp, my noon lunch as my mother used to prepare it, my clothes washed and ironed and laid out for me on the bed, my needs must always take precedence over yours." Can you imagine the likelihood of the success of such a marriage?

On the contrary, Christ died for the sinner, showering the kind of love never ever seen before; he laid down his life for his enemy. *"While we were yet sinners, Christ died for us"* (Romans 5:8). *"Having loved His own who were in the world, He loved them to the end"* (John 13:1). He took the wrath of the law upon himself and satisfied its every demand.

But in his triumphant resurrection he now offers his hand to his bride the church. In a practical application Paul says to the husband: *"Husbands, love your wives, even as Christ also loved the church and gave Himself for it, that He might sanctify and cleanse it with the washing of water by the word, that he might present it to Himself a glorious church, not having spot or wrinkle or any such thing; but that it should be holy and without blemish"* (Ephesians 5:25-27).

We Have Become Dead to the Law   Romans 7:4, 6

This divine truth of our having become dead to the law is a difficult concept to grasp at first reading. The law is, after all, the transcript of God's holiness. The law might appear to be God's answer to the sin question, but Paul had stated earlier: *"For you are not under law, but under grace"* (Romans 6:14). He follows it up in Romans 7 with the illustration of our death in Christ having loosed the bond of the law; then he states clearly on two occasions: *"Therefore, my brethren, you also have become **dead** to the law* [aorist passive-a fact, not a process] *through the body of Christ . . . but now being delivered* ["katargeo"- annulled, loosed, the same word found in Romans 6:6], *from the law, **having died** to what we were held by, so that we should serve in the newness of the Spirit and not in the oldness of the letter."*

We must be clear that the law did not die to us; it remains intact and the sinner must respond to it; rather we died to the power of the law in the body of Christ. Just as in Romans 6: 2, sin did not die to us; its presence remains in the believer, but rather we died to the power of sin over us. It becomes a question of our being released from the demands of the law to please God in the person of the Holy Spirit.

God's Purpose for the Law

The heart of the matter is that in God's plan the law was never meant either to save us or sanctify us. The law demands total absolute compliance with divine perfection with no exception ever granted. *"For as many as are of the* works of the law are under the curse....Christ has redeemed us from the curse of the law, having become a curse for us (for it is written, 'Cursed is everyone who hangs on a tree'") (Galatians 3:10, 13).

God, the Giver of the law, purposed to so convict and convince the sinner of his sin that in total desperation the sinner could only respond to his mercy and grace in the offer of forgiveness and salvation.

In Galatians, an epistle parallel to Romans in so many ways, asks the question: "What purpose then does the law serve? It was added because of transgressions, till the Seed should come to whom the promise was made; and it was appointed through angels by the hand of a mediator" (Galatians 3:19).

Paul concludes that "we [the Jews] were kept under guard by the law, kept for the faith [Christ] which would afterward be revealed. Therefore the law was our tutor to bring us to Christ, that we might be justified by faith" (3:23).The law served a limited purpose for a limited time until the full revelation of Christ, the Seed of the woman, was to come.

Paul makes it clear that the Jew misused the law: "For they being ignorant of God's righteousness, and seeking to establish their own righteousness, have not submitted to the righteousness of God. For Christ is the end of the law for righteousness to everyone who believes" (Romans 10: 3, 4). The correct role of the law was to reduce the Jew and us to repentance and/or reveal our total inability to keep the law, shutting us up to Christ's offer of his grace.

The Anomaly of the Believer and the Law

In the well intentioned hope to become more like Christ, the believer often falls into the trap of trying harder, to imitate *"the meek and lowly of heart."* In the energy of the flesh even the most sincere believer may attempt to respond to the righteous demands of law hoping, in some way, to build merit or to establish his own righteousness. Paul himself on one occasion attempted precisely to respond to the law with the best of intentions - not to covet (Romans 7:7-24). He utterly failed to accomplish the impossible and so will everyone who puts himself or herself under the demands of the law for personal holiness.

The flesh or the self-life has an incessant desire to work, to achieve, to strive to produce self-righteousness. Christian service can be an outlet for self-righteousness: the worthy disciplines of the Christian walk: reading the Bible, time in prayer, sacrificial giving can become devices to impress God or others. Even our efforts toward holiness, any outward effort or inner pride of grace, race or face not grounded in his grace become our filthy rags in this holy presence. *"But we are all like an unclean thing, and all our righteousnesses are like filthy rags; we all fade as a leaf, and our iniquities have taken us away"* (Isaiah 64:6).

Absolutely nothing that originates in the flesh or self, whatever it may claim, can ever please God. *"It is the Spirit who gives life; the flesh profits nothing. The words that I speak to you are spirit, and they are life"* (John 6:63); *"...for without Me you can do nothing"* (John 15:5). *"Because the carnal mind is enmity against God; for it is not subject to the law of God, nor indeed can be. So then, those who are in the flesh cannot please God"* (Romans 8:7, 8). This is God's final pronouncement and ultimatum!

This is a hard lesson to learn. We so often crave some recognition, some rights for ourselves, some justification, some status based on our achievements: academic, missionary, family or success. We justify our failures, excuse our faults, blame others and defend our turf. These are the devices of the flesh that may appear to assuage our sins, but they never will impress our holy God.

We often set up for ourselves artificial norms of conduct, dress, pedigree, standards of our unique group. When we comply with these to our satisfaction, we are proud of our achievements, none of which were God's original norms. Legalism rather than license is often closer to the saint. We compare ourselves with ourselves and are not wise (2 Corinthians 10:12).

Only the Cross is God's answer to Law Keeping

The very essence of the flesh is pride, independence and selfishness. Our manipulations of the law only reveal our baseness. On that basis one cannot build a Christ-like life. The Old and New Testaments are proof positive that God must demolish that fleshly pride. Job defended in exhaustive length his perceived integrity and pride of grace but finally had to say when God himself spoke: *"I have heard of You by the hearing of the ear, but now my eyes see You. Therefore I abhor myself, and repent in dust and ashes"* (Job. 42:5, 6).

Jacob was on the verge of meeting his brother Esau with four hundred men. The crucial moment had come. Jacob alone wrestled with the Angel of Jehovah. The *coup de grace* was when the Angel of the Lord (a theophany, Christ pre-incarnate) asked him: *"What is your name?"* as if he did not know it. When he responded: Jacob or Supplanter (to supplant, deceive by cunning), God gave him a new name, Israel ("for you have struggled with God and with men, and have prevailed.") *"And Jacob called the name of the place Peniel: for I have seen God face to face, and my life is preserved"* (Genesis 32:30).

Moses failed miserably in his first attempt to deliver his people by killing one Egyptian. He needed forty years in the wilderness to undo his proud education (Exodus 2:11-15). When it was God's time, he had no wisdom; he had no ability, but Moses learned where his strength lay. *"Now therefore, go, and I will be with your mouth and teach you what you shall say"* (Exodus 4: 12). His honor was that he became a type of Christ. *"I will raise up from them a Prophet like you from among their brethren, and will put My words in His mouth, and He shall speak to them all that I command Him"* (Deuteronomy 18:18).

Isaiah, the most eloquent of Old Testament prophets, saw the Lord high and lifted up and heard and saw the seraphim proclaim: *"Holy, Holy, Holy is the LORD of Hosts."* Isaiah could do nothing but confess: *"Woe is me, for I am undone! because I am a man of unclean lips, and I dwell in the midst of a people of unclean lips; for my eyes has seen the King, the LORD of Hosts"* (Isaiah: 6:1-7).

The night of Jesus' betrayal Peter had proudly boasted: *"I will lay down my life for Your sake."* And Jesus answered, *"Will you lay down your life for MY sake? Most assuredly, I say to you, the rooster shall not crow till you have denied Me three times"* (John 13:37, 38) We know the story all too well of Peter's denial three times and with cursing. But later he went out and wept bitterly. Our Lord in love told the women to tell the disciples and **Peter** (Mark 16: 7) that he would go before them to Galilee. By the sea of Galilee Jesus restored Peter with a final challenge. A humbled Peter became the spokesman of the early church. A reminder to all of us; there must be a breaking of pride before the reality of the new life can break forth.

But the wonder of God's grace is that we died to the flesh and its infatuation with doing, striving, working in our fleshly effort. God established a new relationship of marriage to another, even to him who was raised from the dead and lives in the heart of the believer. The Christian life is a life of faith motivated by a love relationship with the risen Christ in the power of the Holy Spirit.

Powerful Points to Ponder

1. We died to the law in the body of Christ. We owe the law no duty or striving.
2. *"But he who is joined to the Lord is one spirit with Him"* (1 Corinthians 6:17).
3. Only a divine breaking of the flesh at the cross will suffice for true victory in Christ.
4. Remember it is not our **doing,** but what he **did** and how by faith we appropriate it moment by moment.

Chapter 20

PAUL RESPONDS TO THE LAW, BUT NOT TO GRACE

Romans 7: 7-25

In spite of the liberating truths that Paul has expressed in the preceding verses, Romans 6:1-14 and 7:1-6, he now recounts a past occasion that had haunted him, a sad and tragic reality. As much as he tried, he could not please God nor appease his law's demands.

We can admire Paul for the sheer honesty and openness with which he faced his personal defeat and spiritual sterility. But before God he makes no attempt to justify or modify his failure. He fails and faces it. How can we account for this frustrating experience?

When we read his testimony as a believer, not an unjustified sinner, we see our face reflected in the mirror of God's Word. We, too, have failed and failed often. Paul, not knowing to whom to turn, has just uttered: *"O wretched man that I am! Who will deliver me from this body of death?"* But just as he admits abject defeat, he responds in the very next verse with a shout of triumph: *"I thank God--through Jesus Christ our Lord!"* (Romans 7:24, 25).

Hope has not been betrayed. *"Paul's experience, while the experience of many Christians, is not the Christian experience,"* a quote of L.E. Maxwell that I remember well. I remain forever indebted to my mentor (1942-49) and

Principal of Prairie Bible Institute, to whom I dedicate this book.

A Variety of Interpretations of a Difficult Passage Romans 7:7-24

This passage has been much debated and variously interpreted. Some have said that this is Paul's remembrance of his unsaved days when as a devout Jew he struggled to obey the law. There may have been such moments in his sincerity. However, he said in reference to his earlier days *"concerning the righteousness which is in the law, blameless"* (Philippians 3:6b). That is hardly a concession of defeat as he knew the law in those earlier days. Furthermore, in Romans Paul's argument has been chronological. He left the unbeliever condemned in Romans 3:20.

Others have conjectured that he is speaking in broad general terms about the unbeliever who seeks after God and tries to keep his law. But Paul has consigned the sinner to total condemnation. *"There is none righteous, no, not one. There is none who understands; there is none that seeks after God"* (Romans 3:10, 11).

Some might settle for a "normal" Christian life of struggles, with the ups and downs, and inconsistency. But such a description hardly comports with that usual note of triumph that characterized Paul's life. *"Now thanks be to God who **always** leads us in triumph in Christ, and through us diffuses the fragrance of His knowledge **in every place"*** (2 Corinthians 2:14). *"Yet in **all these things** we are more than conquerors through Him who loved us"* (Romans 8:37).

Paul is speaking in a very personal manner that remembers a past occasion when, as a believer, forgiven of all his sins, he did not grasp by faith the depth of his union with Christ. Knowing doctrinally the truths of the Cross, he as yet had not experienced the barrenness of fleshly endeavor. He did not yet see his sin as *"exceedingly sinful"* (v.13), nor did he *"know that in me (that is, in my flesh) nothing good dwells"* (v.18). But that self-knowledge was to come painfully but finally. In retrospect Paul addresses that moment in all sincerity.

Paul's Encounter with God's Law--The First Step Toward Brokenness   Romans 7:7-13

Paul has just said that he died to the law so as to serve *"in the newness of the Spirit and not in the oldness of the letter"* (v.6). The only problem was that on this occasion he did not experience the newness of the Spirit. He faced his failure, by asking the question: Is the problem with God's law? Evidently not, because God has every right to demand the holiness that he alone can bless. The simple ninth commandment slew him: *"You shall not covet"* (v.7). In effect, he could never ever have any other desire than that of supremely loving and obeying God. The divine demand was an impossible but just command.

His response, as is ours so often, was not to disobey the command but **rather to try to obey.** In itself that intention is commendable; but we just don't have the where-with-all to match the law's demands. So Paul redoubles his effort and the more he strives and tries, the more he fails. That just command would not let him escape its condemnation. The original sin of pride, dependence on self, the principle of the "ego" revived and inflamed and he died.

He could not blame God who had every right to demand perfection as expressed in the law. But the bottom line was:

*"...sin, that it might appear sin, was producing death in me through what is good, so that sin through the commandment might become **exceedingly sinful**"* (v.13). It was God dealing with Paul's sin nature in a deeper way; Paul had no answer but to begin to admit his sin.

God now was using the law in its rightful fashion to reveal the tremendous depth of innate pride and selfishness in his servant. This revelation can never ever be pleasant, but, Oh! how necessary for the subsequent grasp of faith! Paul had not seen his pride before in the light of the law as an expression of God's holiness; he was powerless to deal with that new reality. The process of brokenness had begun and would continue.

Paul's Encounter with God's Law-The Second Step toward Brokenness   Romans 7:14-18

Faced with the condemnation of the exceedingly sinfulness of the "ego" pride, Satan's first sin, Paul analyses correctly that the problem is not with God's law but rather with himself; he is carnal, fleshly in his response to the law. He was not saying that he was carnal in his standing of being justified but rather in practice since he was walking according to the flesh.

Paul now changes from the past tense to the present tense to make more vivid his struggle (vv. 15-25). He is re-living the intensity of effort and corresponding frustration and is drawing on his own best intentions to obey God, as a child of God. But in doing so, he was bypassing God's resources soon to be discovered.

What follows is the sad litany of: *"For what I am doing, I do not understand. For what I will to do, that I do not practice;*

but what I hate, that I do" (v.15). Who has not been there in the inner struggle with a secret sin?

But Paul now arrives at a theologically correct conclusion but still is not fully broken of his self-confidence. The process continues under the tutelage of the Holy Spirit using the law to reveal flesh's total inability to please God. *"For I know that in me (that is, in my flesh) nothing good dwells; for to will is present with me, but how to perform what is good, I do not find"* (v.18).

This admission is a major step toward faith's ability to receive the ministry of the Spirit. The Holy Spirit can only work in us when we allow the Cross to deal with our pride, our root sin. Paul has correctly identified the source of his problem but admits to not knowing how to face it.

Again, who has not been there? The mind of the believer grasps the fact that Christ dwells within. Notice Paul does not deny that good remains in him--a tacit recognition of his regeneration. Christ does dwell in him, but Paul is stymied by the flesh.

Paul's Encounter with God's Law--the Last Step Toward Brokenness   Romans 7:19-24

The struggle continues but negative "progress" is being made. Paul is *"unlearning"* the ways of the flesh, always a most painful process. We must unlearn before we can learn. We must die before we can be raised again. This is the Cross-life that crosses out the "ego" and allows Christ to take his place.

John the Baptist epitomized this truth when he reminded by his disciples that Jesus' appearing on the scene was apparently stealing his disciples. His response to his disciples is classic: *"A man can receive nothing unless it has been given to him from heaven. You yourselves bear me witness, that I said, 'I am not the Christ,' but I have been sent before Him. He who has the bride is the bridegroom; but the friend of the bridegroom, who stands and hears him, rejoices greatly because of the bridegroom voice. Therefore this joy of mine is fulfilled. **He must increase, but I must decrease"** (John 3:25-30).

Paul now faces correctly his dilemma, no "ifs" or "ands" or "buts." *"For I delight in the law of God according to the inward man* [proof positive that Paul experiences this struggle as a believer and an apostle]. *But I see another law* [dynamic, thrust] *in my members warring against the law of my mind, and bringing me into captivity to the law of sin which is in my members"* (vv.22, 23).

Paul is now walking the "treadmill of defeat"; forty-five times he repeats the personal pronouns of "I," "me" and "my" in vv.7-24. No mention is made of the work of the Holy Spirit. Here is self-effort at its best and worst. This is hardly the role of faith!

Paul is rendered powerless, defeated, realizing now that his best endeavors are doomed to failure. Victory in Christ was never the way of self-realization. God had rejected out of hand that concept when he nailed Paul to the cross in Romans 6:6:*"Knowing this, that our old man was crucified with Him, that the body of sin might be done away with* [cancelled, rendered null]*, that we should no longer be slaves to sin."* Paul had not grasped the truth of his union with Christ in living faith and hence his utterly defeated life and that, in spite of all his theological knowledge.

Why is it that this liberating truth is so seldom heard? The Christian is left with the inference, if not the actual requirement, that he should do more: he must try harder, he must imitate, he must do the very best he can. Such a course of action is a prescription for defeat as Paul learned in his sad exclamation.

"O wretched man that I am! Who will deliver me from this body of death?" (v.24). In his utter desperation Paul has finally given up on his own efforts as a possible hope for victory. The answer will not be, Paul but rather WHO? This is progress that will result in divine intervention, never before but always in a timely fashion.

Out of Death Comes the Risen Life   Romans 7:25

Now comes the illumination of the Spirit. Broken of his best intentions and self-righteousness, he must claim by faith his death with Christ, considering himself *"to be dead indeed to sin, but alive to God in Christ Jesus our Lord"* (Romans 6:11).

Watchman Nee in his book, *The Normal Christian Life*, relates a personal experience. He was a conference speaker in Switzerland; one afternoon he was watching the swimmers in the pool. To his consternation he observed a young man going under for the third time. The life guard was passively watching the poor young man. Incensed at such inaction, Nee was blaming the life guard. But in the very last instant of his going down for the third time, the life guard dove into the water and rescued the man in the nick of time.

Later Nee remonstrated with the lifeguard. "Why did you act so late?" He replied: "You don't understand. If I had sought to rescue him while he struggled in the strength of his adrenalin, both of us would have drowned. But when he couldn't struggle any more, he offered no resistance, and the rescue was simple and safe."

God was waiting patiently for Paul to realize that his struggles were futile, useless. There was another way to victory, the way of the Cross, Christ's death and Paul's and yours and mine.

Implicit in Paul's desperate outcry was: WHO, not what or how. Having come to the end of his own resources, he is ready to look away from himself; the Holy Spirit can now bring the truth before known in theory but not grasped in saving faith. I died in Christ to the sin principle; my sin nature so given to pride and effort no longer needs to control me. I look to the Cross and live. We now are prepared to develop the "how" of that crisis moment.

Chapter 21

FROM BROKENNESS TO FULLNESS THROUGH THE HOLY SPIRIT

Romans 7:25 - 8:1, 2

A Quick Survey of Paul's Journey of Faith

Paul has been tracing the role of **Truth, Faith** and **Grace** since he asked that pertinent question in Romans. 6:1: *What shall we say then? Shall we continue in sin that grace may abound?"* His answer rang out: *"Certainly not."* Paul first affirms our *identification* with Christ in our death to the sin principle (6:1-10). He follows that great **Truth** with the role of Faith. He had earlier said: *"It is of **Faith** that it might be according to **Grace**"* (Romans 4:16).

The four step act and attitude of faith follows:

1.) Count yourself dead to sin and alive to God (6:11);

2.) Do not let sin reign (6:12);

3.) Don't be presenting your members as instruments of unrighteousness to sin (6:13 a);

4.) But present yourselves and your members as being alive from the dead (6:13b). Now comes the logical conclusion: *"For sin shall not have dominion over you **for you are not under law but under grace"** (6:14).*

The Christian walk continues. *Grace* is the new relationship that establishes a *"marriage to Another, even to Him who was raised from the dead that we should bear fruit to God"* (7:3). The walk must be in that new love relationship of marriage to the Crucified; we died to the law and its impossible demands. It must be of faith - not striving - that it might be by grace and from that truth of God's grace in Christ issues the wholly new dynamic, the *newness of the Spirit* (v.6).

But Paul's great dilemma was that in that moment his experience of the Christian walk did not quite work out that way! He tried not to covet, he strove, he imitated as best he could, but it led to the *"exceeding sinfulness"* of this inward desire (v.13) which in turn forced him to confess *"in me dwells no good thing* (v.18). Finally *"O wretched man that I am! Who will deliver me from this body of death?* (v.24). Abject failure. We may admire his honesty and effort, but he failed nonetheless. And so it is with every effort of our best endeavor.

Surprised by Grace in Paul's Darkest Moment of Failure
Romans 7:25

There is no quicker turn around in all of Scripture than what Paul now recalls. From the nadir of despair he exalts: *"O wretched man . . . I thank God--through Jesus Christ our Lord"* (7:25) How can this be? He offers no theological explanation; he only affirms a deliverance such that gratitude and praise are the spontaneous responses.

Something must have occurred. No doubt. It had to be the illumination of the Holy Spirit. The light broke through: "I have been trying to do what Christ alone can do. I am attempting to do what He did for me once and for all." Those truths were the truths he "thought he knew" so well and had stated so clearly in Romans 6: 1-14.

But doctrine, as sound as it is, does not itself deliver but only with the humbling of pride by the illumination of the Spirit.

The Holy Spirit responds to that **deeper heart repentance** that grasps in faith the humbling, the breaking of the self-life, that is prerequisite for any of the Spirit's deeper workings.

The above explanation may be considered by some as only an interpretation. But there is a hint of a deeper relationship to Romans 6:6, the Magna Carta of Christian liberty. (This is the famous document signed in 1215 by King John giving the English nobles for the first time a measure of democracy.) In Paul's woeful plea he said: "*Who will deliver me from this **body of death?***" Paul had affirmed in Romans 6:6--my life verse-- "*Knowing this, that our old man was crucified with him that the **body of sin** might be done away with* [rendered null, cancelled] *that we should no longer be slaves to sin.*"

In Romans 6:6 it is the **body of sin** and in 7:25 **this body of death**. Paul simply substitutes the cause for the effect, sin toward death. Paul now knew the moment of his victory and the same for us when we grasp the truth of our union with Christ by simple faith, even in our weakness.

I must make a passing comment to explain the rest of Romans 7:25. It could appear to some that Paul summarizes the rest of his life as an ongoing battle with the flesh: "*So then, with the mind I myself serve the law of God, but with the flesh the law of sin*". Such a conclusion flies in the face of Romans 8:1 and a whole chapter, not of a divided heart but of the fullness of the Spirit. With some 45 references to "I," "my" and "me" to zero references to the Holy Spirit in Romans 7:7-24; now Romans 8 introduces some 21 references to the Holy Spirit; such a conclusion of a double standard of conduct surely does not stand.

In addition, so sudden was the illumination of the Spirit that Paul had to exult in that burst of gratitude. He did not want to take time to summarize the double mindedness evident in his earlier failure in placing himself under the law to which he had died. There may be also an indirect allusion to the rapidity with which one can turn back to the law and the flesh--see Peter's vacillation in Matthew 16:13-23. But with the Spirit's enablement may it never be.

The Triumph of Righteousness through the 'Newness of the Holy Spirit'   Romans 8:1

"There is therefore no"--no kind of legal or moral— *"condemnation to those who are in Christ Jesus."* In the oldest and best manuscripts the rest of the verse does not appear here but does appear correctly in 8:4 where the same phrase finds its rightful place.

This liberating statement is the result of one who in every sense of the word is abiding in Christ, dead to sin and the law and trusting in the love relationship with the Risen Christ. Now the Holy Spirit is in full control and we can be assured of the fullness of forgiveness and abundance of the risen life of Christ. Paul had groaned under the moral self-condemnation of Romans 7:7-24 but now is freed from all kinds of self-condemnation.

Within the context of Romans this statement applies in its fullness to the obedient believer. The verse is often quoted to the recent believer-- which is surely true of the secure standing of justification of the believer. But the context places it clearly in the believer's sanctification or his moral **condition,** his daily walk of faith. This is the strongest statement of the absolute sufficiency of Christ's death and life to be ours in the walk of faith.

Paul returns to the Message of the Cross as the ground of the Spirit's freedom in enabling us to walk in newness of life, in true victory over sin and self. Paul gives us the reason for the freedom. *"For the law of the Spirit of life in Christ Jesus has made* [better as in the original--first aorist active indicative—**made**] *me* [in some versions—you] *free from the law of sin and death."* Paul returns to the cross, the historical fact and the ultimate intervention of the Triune God.

Victory is not something to be achieved in the future, or soon to be attained or when we understand it all. The work was done at the cross and remains done. It is ours to believe and appropriate and truly thank God for. The blessed truths of Romans 8 indeed return us to Romans 6:1-10 and 7:1-6. Nothing can be added to the work already done. Self-effort is futile and useless. Paul had learned that the hard way in the preceding chapter.

In line with that thought Paul continues: *"for what the law could not do in that it was weak through the flesh, **God did** by sending His own Son in the likeness of sinful flesh, on account of sin: He condemned sin in the flesh"* (8:3). Paul continues with the intended result; the righteous requirements of the law of God's character are fully ours by the Holy Spirit. Our co crucifixion with Christ was God's absolute pronouncement that the flesh profits nothing. It is the Spirit who gives life (John 6:63).

God *"condemned sin in the flesh"*--the sin nature, the factory that produces the full range of sinful products (v.3). **The verse is the re-statement of Romans 6:6, our co-crucifixion with Christ**. This vital aspect of his death, so often overlooked today, establishes that he did not die just to forgive our sins and take us to heaven; he died to make available to us the *reign of grace* through the fullness of the Holy Spirit. Such a gift of grace is grounded totally on the work of the Cross.

His condemnation of the flesh involves his final condemnation of my flesh in whatever form it may appear. That work of the Spirit includes my full endorsement of that divine judgment in doctrine and in daily living.

Righteousness or Holiness--the Ultimate End of the Fullness of the Holy Spirit   Romans 8:4

Now God reveals the divine design of his death and resurrection. *"He condemned sin in the flesh, that the righteous requirements of the law might be fulfilled in us who do not walk according to the flesh but according to the Spirit."* If this verse is a re statement of Romans 6, which it is, one can see the intimate relationship with our **knowing and experiencing** that death enabling the Holy Spirit to do his work of releasing the risen life of Christ in us. *"The riches of the glory of this mystery among the Gentiles: which is Christ in you, the hope of glory"* (Colossians 1: 27).

In a similar vein Paul begins his triune doxology with a paean of praise in Ephesians 1: 3 -12: *"Blessed be the God and Father of our Lord Jesus Christ, who has blessed us with every spiritual blessing in heavenly places in Christ, just as He chose us in Him before the foundation of the world, that we should be holy and without blame before Him in love, having predestined us to adoption as sons by Jesus Christ to Himself, according to the good pleasure of His will."*

He died to justify us and to do even more -- to sanctify us by condemning sin in the flesh. The Holy Spirit now becomes the new law in our members to produce in us nothing more or less than the righteous requirements of God's character. This puts into true perspective the fullness of the Spirit—not just to bless us but to produce fruit, the ultimate fruit of Christ-likeness. He died not to make us happy but holy.

A Word of Spiritual Balance

Sadly the doctrine of the Filling of the Holy Spirit or the Fullness of the Spirit, a truth so very important for the believer, is seldom taught from this passage that specifically deals with the Fullness of the Spirit in the life of the believer.

Appeal is so often made to Acts and the phenomena in the early church. On the Day of Pentecost the Holy Spirit did indeed inaugurate the church with credible signs and wonders. However, the book of the Acts is not the paradigm of the Spirit's working. It does indeed reveal the historical features with which God chose to establish the church. The paradigm, however, is the apostolic teaching of the teaching epistles. Romans 8 is the high watermark of that teaching. Here Paul deals with the Holy Spirit as indispensable to the walk of the believer. He develops the role of the Spirit as rooted in the work of the Cross as applied to the believer.

You will notice in this *seminal and primary* passage on the Spirit's ministry, no mention is made of "waiting on the Spirit," "seeking the baptism of the Spirit," no reference to fasting, tarrying to receive the gifts or varieties of experiences but simply to our walk with a crucified Christ.

In fact, Romans 12: 1-21 describes the walk in the Spirit and the gifts of the Spirit in their practical benefit to the church as the Body of Christ. The real test of the fullness of the Holy Spirit is that our walk of faith should glorify the Crucified and Risen Christ, producing in us the holiness and humility that become the true evidence of the fullness of the Spirit, the Holy One.

Live out Thy life within me, O Jesus, King of Kings!
Be Thou Thyself the answer to all my questionings.
Live out Thy life within me, in all things have Thy way!
I the transparent medium Thy glory to display

The temple has been yielded, and purified of sin;
Let Thy Shekinah glory now flash forth from within.
And all the earth keep silence, the body henceforth be
Thy silent docile servant, moved only as by Thee.

Its members every moment held subject to Thy call;
Ready to have Thee use them, or not be used at all.
Held without restless longing, or stain or stress or fret,
Or chafing at Thy dealings, or thoughts of vain regret.

Kept, restful, calm, and pliant, from bond and bias free,
Permitting Thee to settle when Thou hast need of me.
Live out Thy life within me, O Jesus, King of Kings!
Be thou the glorious answer to all my questionings.

France Ridley Havergal

Chapter 22

THE SPIRIT FILLED WALK--WHAT DOES IT LOOK LIKE?

Romans 8: 1-4

A Fuller Perspective on the Walk of Faith

Paul in Romans 8:1- 4 has almost completed his survey of the Christian life as it should be lived. He asked the question: Does the Christian have to sin, to yield to the old Adamic nature? (Romans 6: 1). He answered it sharply – never!

He has given the reason: we died to the First Adam and have been raised to walk in newness of life in the last Adam, Christ. This glorious fact must now be learned and lived by faith. God's work was done at the Cross (v. 6), but ours is to count ourselves dead to sin and alive to God (v. 11); to not let sin reign (v. 12); to not go on yielding to the inertia of the old but rather to present our will and our members to Christ as instruments of righteousness (v. 13). The glorious result is that the sin principle will not reign (v.14).   The sin principle is present but disarmed and annulled.

But one further truth must be grasped. We died to the law, that is, our best self-effort. We are *"married to another, even to Him who was raised from the dead, that we should bear fruit unto God"* (Romans 7:4). This truth Paul himself did not fully grasp on a past occasion but rather turned to his best intentioned self-effort. To Paul's great dismay his "doctrine" did not actually work. His best efforts soon turned into a deeper sense of his sinfulness (v. 13), to the conclusion that no good thing dwelt in him (v.18) and finally to utter desperation: *"O wretched man that I am, who will deliver me from this body of death?"* (v.24).

But as quickly as he gave up on his best self-effort, the liberating truth of his union with Christ filled him with gratitude: *"I thank God – through Jesus Christ our Lord"* (v. 25). This release of the faith principle (6: 11) results in: *"There is therefore no condemnation to those who are in Christ Jesus our Lord"* (8:1).

Paul now gives the reason for his new found freedom: *"For the law of the Spirit of life in Christ Jesus made me free from the law of sin and death"* (8:2). The Holy Spirit who indwells the believer now becomes himself the dynamic of holiness or sanctification. What Paul's best self-effort could never do, the Spirit accomplishes immediately on the basis of Christ's work on the Cross. THIS IS THE MESSAGE OF THE CROSS!

"I have been crucified with Christ; it is no longer I who live, but Christ lives in me; and the life which I now live in the flesh I live by faith in the Son of God, who loved me and gave Himself for me" (Galatians 2:20).

The Simplicity of the Walk of Faith

Paul had learned the hard way; the Christian life is not my best effort but rather a trusting, an affirming of what God did for me in his Son at the Cross, a giving of thanks for it.

Just as in initial salvation, first came a recognition of past sins and present impotency to change, which was followed immediately by the saving work of the Holy Spirit. The Pharisee informed an all-knowing God of all his good deeds; the publican simply cried out: *"God be merciful to me a sinner."* Jesus stated tersely: *"I tell you this man went down to his house justified rather than the other"* (Luke 18:9-14).

No wonder that Paul advises the Colossians: *"Now this I say lest anyone should deceive you with persuasive words....As you have therefore received Christ Jesus the Lord, so walk in Him, rooted and built up on Him and established in the faith, as you have been taught, **abounding in it with thanksgiving"*** (Colossians 2:4, 6, 7). There is a simplicity of faith that confounds the flesh. Paul moved from defeat: *"O wretched man that I am"* to victory: *"I thank God – through Jesus Christ our Lord!"*

Now the Christian Life--Christ-in-Me--Begins   Romans 8:1-4

Tragically so many believers upon receiving Christ by simple faith begin now to imitate him, to try to be like Christ. They set out in their first love and with the new found joy of sins forgiven. But what God did in saving them now becomes to them their "responsibility" to do. Words like: "I should, I must, I'll try, Help me, Lord, to become more like You."

Such responses are well intentioned, but none grasps that glorious fact that He who saved us by grace through faith is the same one who sanctifies us by grace through faith. We have to relearn the lesson that only Christ saves and sanctifies. It is not our doing, but it was his doing at the cross. Paul states again this basic truth so succinctly: ***"As you have therefore received Christ Jesus, the Lord, so walk in Him".*** (Colossians 2: 6) How can we miss so simple a truth!

Dr. F. J. Huegel tells the true story a young believer who found victory in Christ so simply. Dr Huegel was preaching in a church in Cali, Colombia. As usual he was expounding the truths of our union with Christ in death and resurrection, his favorite theme being Romans 6.

After the service a fine looking young man approached him and asked if he could speak with him in confidence. The young man proved to be a student leader in the seminary close by. He poured out his sad story. He was president of the student body; all thought him to be an exemplary spiritual leader. But the reality was that he was a defeated Christian, struggling in the morass of internal conflicts. "**What can I do**?"

Brother Huegel simply went over the steps of Romans 6: You died, God buried the old "I"; he raised you up to walk in newness of life. By faith you go on knowing and believing that simple truth. It is a walk of faith considering yourself dead indeed to sin and alive in Christ. "Let us pray and give thanks for the Cross."

The young man began: "**Lord, help me to do this**. Several times in the prayer: **Help me, Lord.** This was simply the beggar's mentality. After hearing the same words several times, he stopped the young man in mid-prayer. Anyone who knew Brother Huegel knew how gracious he was. But he interrupted the young man's prayer with: "Has God helped you?" "Well, no."

"Let me pray a prayer for you, repeat after me the words but from the heart, not the head." He simply reviewed the truths of the Cross and *gave thanks for the victory already won* and now taken in simple faith. Upon saying: "Amen," he looked at the young man. It seemed that,-- yes, the light was dawning on him: Not by might nor by asking for help but by my Spirit. They embraced in typical Latin fashion and he left satisfied.

But the story does not end there. Within a year Dr. Huegel was back in the same church. A young man entered and

Brother Huegel noted the fact but could not identify him. After the service the young seminary student approached and identified himself. With a simple question from Brother Huegel: "And how goes it? (¿Cómo te va, joven?) He responded: VICTORY!

What had happened was that in his brokenness he simply accepted and had given thanks for what Christ had done and the now the Spirit was doing his work. No doubt that in the intervening year, he may have had a step backward to face the same old "I." But he had entered in by faith. **"Praise and gratitude is faith in full bloom,"** as my mentor often said.

But a footnote, years later I was preaching in the same church the same message. I asked: "How many of you remember Brother Huegel?" Hands went up and faces smiled. The fruit of the Cross.

The Journey Begins with Renewed Anticipation

Let me illustrate these truths by a simple illustration. I personally love to travel; I must be a nomad! In God's providence he has granted me the privilege of ministry in some 17 different countries with some 35 trips to the Caribbean and Central and South America and multiple trips to Mexico. But any simple journey by car to a new destination begins with a map. The map guarantees the route to be taken.

No one invents his own map; he secures the best one he can find. He plans his trips with care. Merely to have the map in hand does not guarantee the safe arrival anywhere. But it is indispensable. God's map for the Christian life is found most clearly in Romans 5:12-8:39. The specific point of departure is Romans 6:6. He develops it, describes it and plots it for us. The tragedy is that so seldom is the truth of Romans 6:6 even mentioned.

God's map reveals where we were in Adam, a sinner (Romans 5:12,) but now we are IN CHRIST, the Last Adam (vv.15-21). It is a **MUCH MORE** relationship. Our point of departure is we DIED to sin in Christ's death (6:1-6); roadside instructions are ours in (vv.11-14). We must not take any side road of self-effort; we DIED to the Law and its impossible demands (7: 1-6). But Paul took a side road of: I'll live the Christian life by my best effort and with God's help (vv.7-24). But he ends up in a cul de sac, a dead end anywhere but his destination. As always, if I'm lost, I must return to my original point of departure which is what Paul does in (v. 25) and is now introduced to the GUIDE who knows the way - the Holy Spirit, the Spirit of Holiness (7:6; 8:1-4)

Recently I was invited to speak at the First Baptist Church (Hispanic) of Reynosa, Mexico, to celebrate Pastor's Day. Pastor Homero Fernández was my former student and now his son, Samuel, was in my class in Theology. Reynosa is only 14 miles from the Institute. In my 59 years at RGBI I have been there innumerable times. I drove directly to the Church. After a 4-hour visit, I was set to return.

I thought I knew the way back to the International Bridge. I tried three times but failed to find the entrance: I was thoroughly confused. In desperation I stopped a man who was cleaning car windows and asked instructions. He offered me his ID and said: "Let me take you there." I did not check his ID and without fear I invited him to get in the car. After all, I knew the language and culture. (Later, my wife was scandalized by such a dangerous suggestion.) He took me a totally new way, recently constructed that I would never have been able to find.

Ultimately I was greatly relieved to see the bridge and gladly gave him a $5.00 tip. A guide who knew the way led me on a new path and I arrived home safely. (Incidentally there was a shootout between the Mexican army and the drug cartel at that hour about 2 miles from the church.)

Our GUIDE is the Holy Spirit and he does his work faithfully. Jesus said: *"He will glorify Me, for He will take of what is Mine and declare it to you"* (John 15: 14). What confidence a Guide who knows the way brings to a new journey!

An Application of How the Christian Life Must Be Lived

We think we know how the Christian life should be lived, but it seems to escape us so often. We put ourselves back under the law; our best self-efforts are bound to fail. We have the map in hand and a true desire in our heart, but we did *"not so learn Christ"* (Ephesians 4:20). Victory comes through our identifying ourselves in his death to sin; then in faith grasping that truth, we allow the GUIDE who dwells within to take us safely on the Walk of Faith.

It is often a painful unlearning process but is followed by greater assurance in the learning process that always results in **"Not I, but Christ."** Christianity is Christ. He lives in us though the power of the Holy Spirit and wants to live out his life of holiness in and through us.

A hymn that expresses so well the overriding characteristic of victory in Christ follows:

> Jesus! I am resting, resting,
> In the joy of what Thou art;

Chapter 22: The Spirit-filled walk--what does it look like?

I am finding out the greatness
of Thy loving heart.
Thou hast bid me gaze upon Thee,
And Thy beauty fills my soul,
For, by Thy transforming power,
Thou hast made me whole.

Chorus
Jesus! I am resting, resting,
In the joy of what Thou art,
I am finding out the greatness
of Thy loving heart.

Oh, how great Thy loving kindness,
Vaster, broader than the sea!
Oh, how marvelous Thy goodness,
Lavish'd all on me!
Yes, I rest in Thee, Belov'd,
Know what wealth of grace is Thine,
Know Thy certainty of promise,
And have made it mine.

Simply trusting Thee, Lord Jesus,
I behold Thee as Thou art,
And Thy love so pure, so changeless,
Satisfied my heart;
Satisfies its deepest longings,
Meets, supplies its ev'ry need
Compasseth me round with blessings:
Thine is love indeed.

Ever lift Thy face upon me,
As I work and wait for Thee;
Resting 'neath Thy smile, Lord Jesus,
Earth's dark shadows flee.
Brightness of my Father's glory,
Sunshine of my Father's face,
Keep me ever trusting, resting,
Fill me with Thy grace.

P.S.Pigott

Chapter 23

THE BELIEVER'S CO OPERATION WITH THE HOLY SPIRIT

Romans 8

Paul sets before us the role of the Holy Spirit as he becomes the indwelling presence of Christ, introducing us in an ever increasing way into our vital union with the crucified Savior. Paul now freed from moral condemnation for his personal failure to live the victorious life (Rom. 7: 7-24) has found the source of constant victory. *"For the law of the Spirit of life in Christ Jesus made me* [us] *free from the law of sin and death"* (8:2).

Paul has given us a new name for the Holy Spirit as the Spirit of life in Christ Jesus. Jesus had spoken of him as Helper or Advocate and the Spirit of Truth (John 14: 16, 17). The Holy Spirit is now the "law" or the dynamic, the motivation of the believer. His **ungrieved presence** supplies us with all we can ever need for a life of fullness in Christ.

Paul has introduced the believer into a new personal and intimate relationship with the Spirit of God. The believer as a member of the Body of Christ is married to a risen Savior (Romans 7:1-6; Ephesians 5:30-32). In one sense, the Spirit has presented us to Christ as our bridegroom. He now lives in us as a person and daily serves as the counselor and guide to develop that relationship.

The Holy Spirit is a person, a divine person, not a force or an impersonal influence. Scriptures speaks of the joy of the Spirit (Acts 13:52) and the love of the Spirit (Romans 15:30). As such we must learn to live with an **open heart to his personality** and his ways of wooing us. After all, he is the Spirit of Christ (Romans 8:9).

My Testimony--A New Personal Relationship with the Holy Spirit

I shall never forget in my first year of Bible school at Prairie [1946-47] at the fall conference, the speaker came with the message of the Spirit's fullness; I had heard and read much about the Holy Spirit as doctrine, but what struck me was that there must be and can be a *welcoming and opening up to his presence within.* Of course, theologically we know that he came to indwell us at salvation and lives in us from that moment. But for so many that is doctrinal data.

The result of the conference was a tremendous movement of the Spirit, a genuine revival in the student body. I was awakened to the reality that the Holy Spirit is a person to be honored, venerated and welcomed exclusively into every facet of my life.

I was in a serious relationship with my girlfriend, now my wife of 63 years; I was, of course, most aware of my desire to cultivate that relationship with her. In this atmosphere of the Spirit's presence and my much deep heart searching, the Spirit spoke to me--no audible voice-- "Do you love me more than GRACE?" "Of course, Lord, I love you more." "Then break the relationship and show me that you do love only me." My cousin roommate assured me that I needed to obey God.

[Incidentally he and his mother were desirous of the change of relationship for obvious reasons!]

I responded and obeyed the Spirit. I sent back the pictures and in a letter simply said that God had spoken to me and had told me to end our relationship. The months that followed were the most fruitful six months of my life. The Holy Spirit became a person to me; he opened up the Scriptures as never before. He gave me two spiritual gifts that ministry since has proven were God-given.

I walked in a new freedom and gladness. That was one of God's deeper dealings with me. I learned that my relationship to the Holy Spirit was worth more than any other human relationship. It is so easy to say: "I love you, Lord," but to offer up "our Isaac" (Genesis 22) is the only proof that we do love him more, and that satisfies God.

Six months later the Spirit said that I was free to begin again the relationship. She agreed. Her response to the Lord had been: "If he loves the Lord more than me, that is a plus, not a minus."

About the same time I was reading a book that changed my perspective on the Christian life. Andrew Murray's book: *The Spirit of Christ*,[15] is a seminal work on the indwelling Spirit. I recall now my memory's non verbatim statement: "The Holy Spirit is a person and we should treat him courteously as we would any other person that we esteem highly. We should venerate him as the Third Person of the Trinity, love him, communicate with him in meditation and prayer. We must at all costs avoid offending him." Since that day I personally pray

---

[15] Andrew Murray, *The Spirit of Christ* (London: Nisbet & Co. Ltd.) 1988) Originally its thirty one chapters were a devotional plus valuable notes in the appendix.

Chapter23: The believer's cooperation with the Holy Spirit

to the Holy Spirit in the specific areas of his scripturally assigned ministries.

I seek never to begin to prepare my heart to speak or write without asking specifically for his anointing, direction and approval. I find myself communing on my bed in the night seasons, as if he were at my side. Such a response enriches immensely the Christian life. This fellowship becomes the essence of the Christian life, not duty, demands and self-effort, but the freshness of an **openness to his persona, presence and approval or disapproval.**

I have a habit, good or bad you may judge, but I often assess a sermon on the mention and the frequency of the recognition of the Holy Spirit's ministry. Recently a pastor spoke on "getting into the Word" in order to grow. He laid it on us "heavy" but there was no mention once of the Holy Spirit's ministry of opening to us the Word. It was to be all our doing. Lesson one--no one should take the Word in hand without a prayer to the Holy Spirit: open my heart to your Word and your Word to my spirit.

Biblical Counsels to Honor His Person

Since the Christian life is a daily walk with all the varying ups and downs of life, the Bible does counsel us to avoid offending the Holy Spirit. The classic passage is Paul's terse commands: *"Rejoice always, pray without ceasing, in everything give thanks; for this is the will of God in Christ Jesus for you. Do not quench the Spirit. Do not despise prophecies. Test all things; hold fast what is good. Abstain from every form of evil. Now may the God of peace Himself sanctify you completely; and may your whole spirit, soul and body be preserved blameless at the coming of our Lord Jesus Christ. He who called you is faithful, who also will do it"* (Thessalonians 5:16-24). What a classic exhortation to allow the Spirit of Christ to dwell in us richly! Everything that pertains to holy living pertains directly to the Spirit.

Above all else, he is the <u>Holy Spirit.</u> He knows our secret thoughts, the secret areas that no one else knows. Therefore we must constantly recur to the cleansing of the blood. No one is exempt from secret emotions and reactions, desires, habits and carryovers from the fleshly life.

David said it better than anyone: *"Search me, O God, and know my heart: try me and know my anxieties; and see if there is any wicked way in me, and lead me in the way everlasting"* (Psalm 139:23, 24). Again, *"Who can understand his errors? Cleanse me from secret faults. Keep back Your servant from presumptuous sins. Let them not have dominion over me . . . Let the words of my mouth and the meditation of my heart be acceptable in Your sight, O LORD, my strength and my redeemer"* (Psalm 19:12-14). Incidentally Dr. Huegel had the habit of virtually always beginning his message with the prayerful quoting of the last verse. What a memory to retain!

A Parallel Passage on the Fullness of the Spirit Ephesians 5:18-6:20

The passage of Romans 8:1-4 is clearly the first and foremost mention of the fullness of the Holy Spirit. That passage is the continuum of the argument that the work of the Cross is a whole unit involving our death to sin, to the law that now permits the Holy Spirit to do his work of filling and empowering. However, Romans 8:3, 4 is **not a command to be filled,** but a statement telling us "how" and "why" the

Spirit fills us and does his work of holiness in life and service. It is a purpose clause in the subjunctive mood.

Paul subsequently in Ephesians expounds the very same basic truths. He outlines that we were dead in trespasses and have been made alive (Ephesians 2:5) and that God has raised us up to sit in heavenly places (v.6). Paul devotes chapter 4 to the "how" of the Christian life: *"Put off the old man . . . and be renewed in the spirit of your mind"* (vv.22, 23). He exhorts the believer to *"walk worthy"* (4:1), to *"walk in love"* (5:2), *"to walk circumspectly"* (5:15) and then he caps it off: *"And do not be drunk with wine, in which is dissipation; but be filled with the Spirit"* (Ephesians 5:18).

The best rendering of the command to be filled is in the present passive imperative mood of not being filled with wine but now rather to *"be being filled."* It is not a command for an initial or a definite filling but rather a **being continuously filled,** grounded in our union with Christ and his Cross-work. It is an ongoing infilling that leads to discretion, discipline and holiness and not to dissipation and "spiritual pride".

Immediately Paul applies that truth to such a filling which is now characterized by gratitude, joy and singing (vv.19, 20). He says it will issue in submission to one another (v. 21). Without mentioning signs, wonders, miracles, prophecies or any given experience, he says it transforms the marital relationships (vv. 22-33), the family duties (6:1-4) and society's demands (vv.5-9). Furthermore it fits us to do spiritual warfare and live in victory over Satan and demon forces (vv.10-20).

Interestingly enough another prison epistle has an exactly parallel passage (Colossians 3:1-4:1) that substitutes the filling of the Spirit with: *"Let the word of Christ dwell in you richly in all wisdom, teaching and admonishing one another in psalms and hymns and spiritual songs, singing with grace in your hearts to the Lord."* (Colossians 3:16). The Spirit and the Word come together to make for a life ordinary and extraordinary in love for God and service to others.

A Word of Clarification and Caution.

So much has been written about the Fullness of the Spirit, the experience of the "Baptism of the Spirit," the gifts of the Spirit, the charismatic expression of these last decades that confusion so often reigns. A pseudo spirituality is often professed, signs and wonders are lauded, apostles and prophets appear, prophecies and visions have been claimed and the body of Christ often has been divided into separate camps.

Let it be said the God is sovereign and may give to one believer or to another a personal experience that is somewhat unique. Any given experience can never in itself be what authenticates a work of God. The history of God's dealing with his servants bears out this fact. But paramount to everything is the rule of the Word of God and its clear exposition and our submission to its authority. The inspired Word is always the plumb line of truth.

In divine wisdom God's Word sets the standard and norm, not any given experience, be it genuine or not; given in a unique way to one it is never a pattern for all. God is free to do his work in his way, but what he gives will never contradict the written Word of God properly understood. The proof of the Spirit's authenticity is the mark of Christ-likeness, personal holiness as defined in character, not only in externals and ministry. Ultimately the fullness of the Spirit will reveal itself in humility, love and passion for God and his missionary cause in this world.

The real tragedy is that this confusion has allowed Satan to deprive the church of so much of the Spirit's power. Other crucial passages are not given their rightful place, such as, Romans 6-8; Galatians 2-6; Ephesians 4-6; Colossians 2, 3; 1 Corinthians 12-14; 2 Corinthians 2:14--6:10; 1 John and James. These passages give the "how," the "why" and the "when" of the Spirit's work.

For many the Book of the Acts has been made the cornerstone of the doctrine of the Holy Spirit. Indeed, doctrine may be taught by illustration in Acts; Luke does give us accurately what happened without generally giving us the "why" and the "how." The Spirit's phenomena are generally treated historically and not theologically.

The unnecessary divorce between the Acts and the Epistles has led to different emphases and conclusions. *A true rule of thumb is that the Epistles interpret for us the Acts of the Apostles.* There can be no discrepancy between them. The Holy Spirit is author of both portions of the Inspired Word. We will see the role of the walk of faith, either after the Spirit or after the flesh. God will only bless the former, not the latter.

Chapter 24

TWO SHARP CONTRASTS - THE FLESH AND THE SPIRIT

Romans 8: 5-8

In Romans 8:5-9 Paul is moving toward the climax of a Spirit-filled life. But the Spirit guides Paul to face squarely the options of the believer who may walk according to the flesh. In one sense this is not a valid option for the believer who has died to the flesh (Romans 6:6); but such a result may be a choice through ignorance or disobedience to the Spirit. What began in Romans 5:12-21 as our basic oneness with the Last Adam as opposed to the First Adam is still the ground for not continuing to live in sin.

The question of Romans 6:1: *"Shall we continue in sin...?"* That question has now been fully answered. Rather we died to sin in Christ when he died once for all to sin. Paul has outlined the steps of faith in Romans 6: 2, 6, 10-14.

The next major step was our death to the Law, as if our best self-efforts could possibly suffice to bring us victory over sin. (Romans 7:1-6) God's remedy is our spiritual union or marriage to a Risen Christ who brings the person and power of the Holy Spirit to meet our deepest needs.

Paul failed miserably on one occasion to grasp this truth by faith, rather he insisted on trying to imitate Christ and master his sinful desires. Out of this painful experience now past, he realizes the breaking process needed to cast himself altogether on the Crucified. But just as suddenly as he "broke" before the Lord: *"O wretched man that I am! Who will deliver me from this body of death?"* (v.24), he breaks out in a cry of victory. *"I thank God –through Jesus Christ our Lord!"* (v.25).

He has returned to his true position, dead to sin and alive to Christ. Within this context of faith, the Holy Spirit freed (past tense) him to now fulfill in him the *"righteous requirements of the Law"* (8:4).

The Absolute Polarities of the Flesh and the Spirit
Romans 8:5-8

Paul now appears to interrupt his development of the ministry of the Holy Spirit in order to put into acute relief the incompatibilities of the flesh *vis a vis* the Spirit. In reality, Paul continues his emphasis on the *"walk according to the Spirit"* by describing the positive aspects of the Holy Spirit's "modus operandi" (methods *of* operation) in the believer.

Such is his link with Romans 8:1-4. However, he has just finished relating that occasion when he did not walk according to the Spirit (7: 7-25). His best efforts to "not covet" proved a dismal failure. There is, therefore, the possibility of an abnormal practical relationship with the indwelling sin nature.

Paul concedes that abnormal possibility but gives it no legitimate weight in view of our position in Christ.

Rather, Paul puts into sharp relief the polarities of the flesh and Spirit. There can be no collusion or complicity between the two. In regard to the **legal position of justification** there is absolutely no link between the flesh and Spirit; we stand justified once and for all in Christ. But as to the **practical condition of sanctification or personal holiness,** Paul will admit the possibility of a lapse in the believer's walk of faith, even within the confines of Romans 8, a chapter devoted to victory.

The sharp contrast between these two modus operandi is highlighted and is seen most distinctly in the unbeliever as opposed to the believer. Such is the unbeliever's lost position before God. There is a basic difference of **orientation** – *"For those who live according to the flesh set their minds on the things of the flesh, but those who live according to the Spirit"* (v.5); there is a basic difference of **result** – *"For to be carnally minded is death, but to be spiritually minded is life and peace"* (v.6).

There is a basic difference of essence-- *"Because the carnal mind is enmity against God; for it is not subject to the law of God, nor indeed can be. So then, those who are in the flesh [as to their legal standing] cannot please God"* (vv.7, 8).

This final conclusion is a categorical imperative to be borne in mind, even by the believer who has worked to serve God but in the energy of the flesh. For every believer this is a solemn warning. The Judgment Seat of Christ will be the final resolution of much service rendered in his name but not in the Spirit.

Our Lord himself introduced the essential polarities of the flesh and Spirit when he confronted Nicodemus with the startling statement. Nicodemus was the best known rabbi and teacher in Israel, but in that confrontation Jesus deflected Nicodemus' assumed equal position to the one whom he called "Rabbi." Our Lord's response must have confounded him. *"Most assuredly, I say to you* [plural, a reference to the Pharisees] *unless one is born again, he cannot see the kingdom of God"* (John 3:3).

In the face of Nicodemus' confusion Jesus repeats without explanation the same response: *"Most assuredly, I say to you, unless one is born of water and the Spirit, he cannot enter the kingdom of God. That which is born of the flesh is flesh. And that which is born of the Spirit is spirit. Do not marvel that I said to you, 'You must be born again [born from above]'"* (vv.5-7).

Our Lord would later set forth the infinite love of God for the world (John 3:16) as manifested in Christ who came not to condemn the world but that the world might be saved (John 3:17). Nicodemus will later understand that saving truth when he helps in the burial of our Lord (John 19:39).

Paul Draws the Practical Conclusions in the Life of the Believer

Paul's declaration of the polarities underscores the full privilege of the believer to walk according to the Spirit. At the same time he is realistic enough to know that the walk of faith is a maturing, a learning and "unlearning" process.

In his letter to the Galatians written about the same time as his letter to the Romans, he sets forth the reality of the walk of faith. There is a practical tension and conflict between the Spirit and the flesh. *"I say then: Walk in the Spirit, and you shall not fulfill the lusts of the flesh. For the flesh lusts against the Spirit, and the Spirit against the flesh; and these are contrary to one another, so that you do not the things that you wish. But if you are led by the Spirit, you are not under the law"* (Galatians 5: 16-18).

Paul follows with the enumeration of the works of the flesh and concludes by saying: *"Of which I tell you beforehand, just as I told you in the past, that those who practice such things will not inherit the kingdom of God"* (5:21). These polarities ultimately define the unbeliever as opposed to the believer.

The Christian cannot practice sin with impunity. He may sin, but it is not his new and true nature. If he should sin there are the consequences of losing fellowship with his Lord. John states the same truth *"Whoever is born of God does not* [practice] *sin, for His seed remains in him; and he cannot* [practice] *sin because he has been born of God"* (1 John 3:9).

Paul returns in Galatians 5 to the "Normal Christ Life" by listing the fruit of the Spirit (vv.22, 23) and concludes *"And those who are Christ's **have crucified the flesh** with its passions and desires. If we live in the Spirit* [our new standing] *let us walk in the Spirit"* (v.25). This is the true Christian life to be lived in our mortal body. On this basis Paul will proceed to give his summary (Romans 8:9-13).

However, a good dose of reality follows in Galatians 5: *"Let us not become conceited, provoking one another, envying one another"* (v.26). In the next chapter he gives us as believers a solemn reminder: *"For he who sows to his flesh will of the flesh reap corruption, but he who sows to the Spirit will reap everlasting life"* (6:8).

The believer must learn the disturbing realty of the depth of his Adamic nature. In the popular culture it is "I'm OK and You're OK." The depths of our depravity are seldom plumbed.

I recall singing from memory in my adolescence in our small holiness mission in Winnipeg, Manitoba, Canada, a hymn that challenged me greatly:

> Search me, O God! My actions try, and let my
> life appear

As seen by Thine all-searching eye, to mine my
ways make clear.

Search all my sense, and know my heart who only
canst make known,
And let the deep, the hidden part to me be fully
shown.

Throw light into the darkened cells where passion
reigns within;
Quicken my conscience till it feels *the
loathsomeness of sin*.

Search all my thoughts, the secret springs, the
motives that control;
The chambers where polluted things hold empire
oér my soul.

Search, till Thy fiery glance has cast its holy light
through all,
And I by grace am brought at last before Thy face
to fall.

Thus prostrate I shall learn of Thee what now I
feebly prove,
That God alone in Christ can be Unutterable love.

F. Bottome

However, even in a cursory reading of the lives of the saints,
there has been an ever deepening need for God's light of

holiness to shine into the darker recesses of our being, areas often even unknown to ourselves. For that reason Paul lists the wide variety of the sins of the flesh and warns the believer to look deeply inside. There is a full provision in Christ and the work of the Cross. The Holy Spirit must do his work of revealing **the loathsomeness of sin**. This is not mere introspection but illumination of our wholeness of Christ in us.

To the Corinthians Paul reveals our proper response to the work of the Spirit: *"But we all, with unveiled face, beholding as in a mirror the glory of the Lord, are being transformed into the same image from glory to glory, just as by the Spirit of the Lord. Therefore, since we have this ministry, as we have received mercy, we do not lose heart. But **we have renounced the hidden things of shame,** not walking in craftiness nor handling the word of God deceitfully, but by manifestation of the truth commending ourselves to every man's conscience in the sight of God"* (2 Corinthians 3:18; 4:1, 2). What a challenge to our casual living!

As Watchman Nee has said so concisely, the blood of Christ is efficacious for the forgiveness and cleansing of our sins and the Cross of Cross for victory over the power of the sin nature. No wonder August M. Toplady in his hymn "Rock of Ages" says so eloquently:

Rock of Ages, cleft for me, let me hide myself in
Thee!
Let the water and the blood, from thy riven side
which flow'd,
Be of sin the double cure, cleanse me for its guilt
and power.

Not the labours of my hands can fulfil thy law's demands;
Could my zeal no respite know, could my tears for ever flow,
All for sin could not atone; Thou must save and Thou alone.

Nothing in my hand I bring, simply to Thy cross I cling:
Naked, come to Thee for dress; helpless, look to Thee for grace;
Foul, I to the fountain fly; Wash me, Savior! Or I die!

Chapter 25

THE ULTIMATE BALANCE IN THE LIFE OF VICTORY

Romans 8: 9-13

A Further Review to Better Understand the Context

Paul brings us at last to the final statement of sanctification as a walk of faith grounded in our new **position** (justification) and our new **condition** (regeneration) in Christ. With the sharp contrasts of the polarities of the flesh and Spirit, highlighted in Romans 8:5-8, Paul has inferred the possibility of the believer's abnormality of yielding to the flesh, but Paul makes crystal clear there is neither license to sin nor demand to sin.

God follows up theologically our justification with the regenerating work of the Holy Spirit by which the love of God is poured forth by the Holy Spirit who was given to us in Romans 5:5-8. Simultaneously with justification, God grants eternal life, the very quality of the risen life of Christ (cf., the Bridge, 5:9-11). Christ's resurrection is our guarantee of that eternal life that makes possible the ever deepening work of sanctification. Sanctification becomes the evidence of justification.

Paul has moved through our identification with Christ in death to sin and resurrection life (6:1-14). He followed up this point of departure with four simple steps of faith and thanksgiving that result in freedom from sin's power over the believer (vv.10-14).

Next Paul deals with the dynamic of victory, the person of the Holy Spirit. We are married to a risen Christ *"so that we should serve in the newness of the Spirit and not in the oldness of the letter"* (7:4-6).

To our great surprise, however, instead of the victory as expected, he confesses to his sincerity in trying to meet the righteous demands of the law, his deep struggle and finally abject defeat. But from that occasion he learned how NOT to live the life of victory in Christ (vv.13-24). In total brokenness and frustration, he grasps his position in Christ. In an act of the Spirit's illumination, he exclaims: *"I thank God—through Jesus Christ, our Lord!"* (v.25a).

After this outburst of faith he states the "how" of victory: *"The law of the Spirit of life in Christ **made me** [us - past tense] free from the law of sin and death."* In the briefest of terms he summarizes the basic point of departure for the believer, that is, Romans 6:1-6. *"For what the law could not do in that it was weak through the flesh, **God did** by sending His own Son in the likeness of sin flesh, on account of sin: He condemned sin in the flesh"* (8:3).This is Romans 6:6 restated in the context of the presence and power of the Holy Spirit to do his sanctifying work.

As Paul begins to finalize the contrasting polarities of flesh and Spirit (8:5-8), he draws a firm line between the unbeliever and the believer. But he does grant the anomaly of fleshly responses when the believer does not walk in faith and obedience to the Word. All believers must eventually face the unknown depths of the self-life, but he can take them to the Cross to be set aside. Most sadly these responses are seen too often in our own hearts; they often abound among us. Witness the anger, deceit, envy, jealousy, divisions and even moral lapses that are almost commonplace even among missionaries.

Paul's Declaration of Victory in the Face of the Reality of Indwelling Sin

With this survey of progressive truth, keep in mind that Paul now declares in the boldest of terms the total adequacy of our union with Christ. Time and again Paul has stated the truth of the efficacy of the Cross. Notice the frequency of his position and the clarity of the question. *"Shall we continue in sin that grace may abound? Certainly NOT!"* Then the logical consequence: *"How shall we who died to sin, live any longer in it?"* By no stretch of the imagination can the sin nature ultimately rule; neither logic nor reality can deny our death to self and so impugn the work of the Cross.

Again after Paul has placed clearly before his readers the four steps of moment by moment victory: 1) **count** yourself dead indeed to sin and alive to God; 2) **don't let sin reign;** 3) **stop presenting** your members to sin and 4) **present yourself** to God; then sin will not have dominion over you (Romans 6:11-14). These steps are crucial affirmations often overlooked. Then and only then, he goes on to challenge the reader with: Whom you obey, you are a servant, whether sin unto death or of obedience unto righteousness. This premise is undeniable, but is followed up by exclamations of gratitude.

How does he respond? *"But God be thanked that though you were slaves of sin, yet you obeyed from the heart that form of doctrine to which you were delivered . . . But now having been set free from sin, and having become slaves of God, you have your fruit unto holiness and the end, everlasting life"* (6:17,22). Paul recognizes the genuine work of the Cross in the believer.

Again in introducing the person and work of the Holy Spirit, Paul affirms the truth, our spiritual union that guarantees fruit to God, to serve in the newness of the letter. But to our surprise what follows is a pitiful tale of defeat and frustration. But again the illumination of the Spirit brings the reality of his work in response to faith.

All of this review is to show that Paul is convinced of the absolute reality of victory in Christ. But he is realistic enough to know that the believer will face a self-life impossible to deny. While he grants the presence of self, he denies its right to reign.

Paul Affirms Victory in Christ   Romans 8:9-11

As Paul approaches his summary of Christ's victory over **the law of sin and death** first introduced in Romans 7:23; 8:2, he makes a categorical statement with no ifs, ands or buts. ***"But you are not in the flesh but in the Spirit"*** (v.9). So convinced is Paul of this truth that he makes it a starkly either/or situation. There is no third way. Either a non-believer, an enemy of God's righteousness or a believer and standing in the full dress of that righteousness.

He bases this certainty on a premise long established: *"the love of God was poured out in our hearts by the Holy Spirit who was given to us"* (5: 6). While the word "if" does appear, it is a condition of the first class assumed by impeachable authority to be true. The conjunction "since" would better state the reality that the Spirit of God is the "crown jewel" of salvation and constitutes it and empowers it.

Paul now states the opposite and the obvious: *"Now if anyone does not have the Spirit of Christ, he is not His"* (v.9). Nothing can be clearer. The Holy Spirit is a living person and cannot be divided into portions or stages of human experiences. He may not have practical control over all areas of our life and in that sense we may hinder his full working. But he is ours "to have and to hold from that day forward."

Paul has systematically dealt with what he discovered in Romans 7 – the reality of the **"law of the sin and death."** *"For what the law could not do in that it was weak through the flesh, **God did** by sending His own Son in the likeness of sinful flesh, on account of sin: He condemned sin in the flesh"* (v.3). Paul has nullified the first two; God's law in Christ has been fully vindicated, but our best efforts to keep the law only further provoked the sin nature which was judged once for all at the Cross.

Now Paul will deal with the **body of sin** (Romans 6:6): *"And if Christ is in you, the body is dead because of sin, but the Spirit is life because of righteousness"* (v.10). Once again it is Christ, God's present answer, even for our mortal bodies. Christ in us guarantees our resurrection body, a glorified body given to us in his future presence. *"But if* [or since] *the Spirit of Him who raised Jesus from the dead dwells in you, He who raised Christ from the dead will also give life to your mortal bodies through His Spirit who dwells in you"* (v.11).

Even though the mortal body may be a "drag" on our walk of faith, the Spirit's power can offset those limitations and grant us power to resist their inertia. Here and now resurrection power is ours to claim. The future resurrection body is included as a certainty. Paul has covered all the bases to show the triumph of the Cross over every aspect of sin, past, present and future.

Some interpreters have suggested that this quickening of the body refers to physical healing. But the context does not introduce that truth. Paul has elsewhere stated that *"the body is for the Lord and the Lord for the body"* (1 Corinthians 6:12, 13).

But before he finalizes his appeal in the succeeding verses, it is especially worthy to take note of the repetition and variation of the names of the Triune God. First, there is the Spirit of God (v.9a), then the Spirit of Christ (v.9b), then Christ himself (v.10a), then the Spirit himself (v.10b), then the Spirit of him who raised Jesus (v.11a), and finally through His Spirit who dwells in you (v.11b).

Paul's Solemn Summary and Challenge   Romans 8:12, 13

The journey to true holiness began in Romans 3:21-26. Paul established the basis of our sanctification in Romans 6 where he declared our identification with Christ in death and resurrection followed by the three steps of faith (vv.11-14); later in Romans 7 he introduced our spiritual marriage to a risen Christ to "serve in the newness of the Spirit." In Romans 8 the presence and power of the Holy Spirit is our guarantor of victory.

We come to the final "therefore"--the consequence of believing faith and dependence on the Spirit. His pronouncement is authentic and demanding. *"Therefore, brethren, we are debtors--but not to the flesh, to live according to the flesh. For if you live according to the flesh you will die"* (v.13). Such a direct statement is by no means meant to indicate the loss of our salvation after so much positive teaching to the contrary.

Very much on the contrary Paul wants to drive home in the sharpest terms forever that that end is not the calling of the believer. Paul wants to grab our attention with the strongest negative possible. That debtorship to the flesh ended in Romans 1:18-3:20; it ended at the Cross.

In a similar vein, in his introduction, Paul openly classified himself: *"I am debtor both to Greeks and barbarians, both to wise and unwise. So, as much as is in me I am ready . . . ."* (1:14, 15). In the same vein we are debtors to holiness, to God who paid such a staggering price in the death of his Son and has provided everything *"for life and godliness."*

Now in the briefest summary possible Paul sets forth the "how" of true abiding victory. Mark carefully the syntax, the emphasis of his rejoinder: ***"but if by the Spirit you put to death the deeds of the body, you will live"*** (8:13b). The very first order of business is to realize that the person and power of the Holy Spirit is the dynamic, the fountainhead of the truth of our union with Christ. The Christian life started with his being given to us (Romans 5:5). Victory will never ever be our doing in any meritorious way.

But there is an important corollary that enables the Spirit to do his liberating work. Whenever he sees our faith agreement with God's judgment on the flesh, when we say a cordial Amen to the work of the Cross, the Holy Spirit fulfills in us the *"righteous requirement"* of the law. Where faith in our union with Christ is seen, the Holy Spirit is doing his work of grace.

> Church of God, belov'd and chosen,
> Church of God for whom Christ died,

Claim thy gifts and praise the Giver!
"Ye are washed and sanctified!"
Sanctified by God the Father,
And by Jesus Christ His Son,
And by God the Holy Spirit,
Holy, holy Three in One.

By his will He sanctifieth,
By the Spirit's power within;
By the loving hand that chast'neth,
Fruits of Righteousness to win;
By His truth, and by His promise,
By the Word, by His gift unpriced,
By His own blood, and by our union
with the risen life of Christ.

Holiness by faith in Jesus,
Not by effort of thine own,
Sin's dominion crushed and broken,
by the power of grace alone;
God's own holiness within thee,
His own beauty on thy brow,
This shall be thy pilgrim brightness,
This thy blessed portion now.

He will sanctify thee wholly;
Body, spirit, soul shall be
Blameless 'till thy Savior's coming
In His glorious majesty!
He hath perfected forever
those whom he hath sanctified;

Chapter 25: The Ultimate Balance in the Life of Victory

Spotless, glorious and holy
Is the Church, His chosen Bride.

Frances Ridley Havergal (1836-1879)

Chapter 26

THE HERITAGE OF LIFE IN CHRIST--GUIDANCE AND THE SPIRIT'S WITNESS

Romans 8:14-17

To appreciate fully the blessings that follow in Romans 8:14 and onward, the believer must learn to live by the previous scriptural context that guarantees the blessed results of victory in Jesus. We cannot walk after the flesh and expect to know victory in Christ. The Holy Spirit grieved (Ephesians 4:30), quenched (1 Thessalonians 5:19) and resisted (Acts 7:51) cannot grant the full blessings of Romans eight. After all, the Holy Spirit is the dynamic of the abundant life and he is characterized by holiness. Only the ever deepening work of the Cross can free the Holy Spirit to do his liberating work of grace in us.

The Highlights of the Spirit's Work

What are the conditions of obedience required to receive the inestimable blessings listed in Romans 8? All too often we claim the blessings of chapter 8 without knowing and obeying the truths of chapters 5-7. God does give his blessings in grace, not on our merit but on his mercy. He is "*the Father of mercies and the God of all comfort* [encouragement]." (2 Corinthians 1:3). But we cannot presume on his mercies when God has provided the grace to walk "*according to the Spirit* and not according to the flesh." The manifestations of the flesh, however, are all too often the sad reality in many believers. But in no way is the believer a *"debtor to the flesh to live after the flesh"* (Romans 8:4, 12, 13).

Romans 8 is a life of victory, not a false triumphalism but rather a walk of simple faith and obedience conditioned on a walk *"according to the Spirit."* God's gifts given in grace become the marks of that balanced walk: *"But if **by the Spirit** you put to death the deeds of the body, you will live"* (8:13).These blessings, then, become the distinguishing features of the believer.

Blessings And Characteristics of the Spirit's Work   8:14-17
Uniquely Guided by the Spirit   Romans 8:14, 15

Paul introduces the first blessing and mark of the believer — the availability of guidance and direction at any given moment of life. What question is most frequently asked: How can I know the will of God? Usually our urgency to know is the immediate need to not make a false choice. Such an attitude may reveal ascertain indolence in the walk of faith. Since we live by faith and not by sight, the right step will be the next step of faith in the Spirit's time table. He gives the needed guidance according to his time table, not ours. Panic and fear are not factors in guidance. Our urgency to know may not be his urgency to reveal.

A personal note: while in Prairie Bible Institute, I was assigned, as a special graduation speaker, the topic: **Guidance and the Will of God.** I would have been hardly 21 years of age; what would I know about guidance? I remember meeting with Miss Ruth Dearing, a rather imposing long time teacher, to discuss the topic. I had 15 minutes to fill and what was I to say?

I can claim no inspiration but the main thought that God brought to mind was. **You choose in faith and commit to specific obedience to the will of God,** whatever it may prove finally to be; that acceptance and commitment to obey without knowing what it may be is of essence and will be played out in God's timing. *"If any one wants to do His will, he shall know . . ."* (John 7:17). It may require a wait, a possible "rejection," a step of sheer faith, but it will eventually carry God's imprimatur.

In 1954 God's call to us for missionary service at Rio Grande precisely followed that pattern: a definite call to missions and teaching, a rejection by a well-known mission board because of my wife's health--apparently excellent--a "wait" and then a step of obedient faith to leave Winnipeg with two young daughters without significant financial support. Some thought that this course of action was sheer folly.

But God knew that in that perplexing time of waiting, he was preparing my heart through a breaking of my "spiritual" pride. After that humbling experience that gave new direction to my life, we were living in a revival state of heart, just waiting and serving God where we were; the Spirit was doing his gracious work of gradual confirmation. We have never looked back on that crisis moment.

A divine axiom is that you cannot walk in the flesh in small matters and then expect God to guide you by his Spirit in larger matters. In matters large and small, we must learn to walk by faith according to the Spirit and not the flesh. J. Stuart Holden has said: "Faith and the will of God are inseparable."

A word of caution is also in place. The Spirit's guidance is suited uniquely to the believer that he is guiding. You cannot follow another's example, no 5 or 7 steps to know the will of God. Clearly there are Biblical principles at play: a walk of faith, short accounts with God, counsel of spiritual peers and the interaction of providential circumstances. But ultimately in that given moment, it is the believer's openness to the Spirit and a heart attitude of faith and submission that brings God's assurance.

It is no coincidence that Paul follows the promise of his guidance of the Spirit with a reference to our adoption as his full-fledged sons. God has raised the believer far above the angelical powers that stand in his very presence. *"For you did not receive the spirit of bondage again to fear, but you received the Spirit of adoption by whom we cry out, 'Abba, Father'"* (v.15). Our sense of need for guidance on our terms is often so demanding that fear and anxiety take precedence over the surety of our standing in union with Christ as adopted sons.

The doctrine of adoption is a Pauline concept grounded in God and in Roman culture. (Cf., Romans 8:23; 9:4; Galatians 4:5; Ephesians 1:5). The Hebrew culture knew of no such equality and privilege given to a foreigner or slave. In Paul's day a Roman slave without any claim to sonship could be adopted by the action of the citizen father. To the adopted son would be granted the very same standing of privilege and inheritance as to the natural born son. What a parallel to God's infinite grace in suggesting that we cry out, *"Papi, Father!"* That childlike first word almost seems sacrilegious to our ears. But such is the right of full spiritual sonship.

There is one further interesting note to compare. *"And because we are sons, God has sent forth the Spirit of His Son into our heart, crying out, 'Abba, Father'"* (Galatians 4:6). Possibly Paul's personal Aramaic background *"Abba,* Father" comes to the fore in place of the Hebrew correctness. In comparing Romans and Galatians there is a veritable chorus of the two witnesses, the Spirit himself and the believer respond in one accord claiming intimacy and availability. What confidence we have in approaching the Spirit with our need for guidance!

A theological aside may suggest that God created the angelic world to do his bidding and stand in his presence to worship and extol his wonders. God never planned to redeem the fallen angels; he reserved them in chains in outer darkness. But God had a higher purpose in creating man in his image and likeness. He was to raise him to be joined to his own Son; the reason for the intervention of sin in God's ultimate plan was for God to show his infinite love and righteousness in removing the sin stain and establish through adoption the far higher standing for the forgiven believer. Now we see the matchless marvel of divine grace and the infinite cost to God himself to raise us to be able truthfully to say: *"Papi,* Father."

Uniquely given is the Witness of the Spirit   Romans 8:16, 17

A major blessing now made known to us is the access or the **witness of the Holy Spirit to our spirit.** For so many of us, we are often stone deaf to our own spirit, the channel that God gives to us to access the presence of the Holy Spirit. In regeneration he quickened our spirit once dead in sin in order to become his channel to us for true spiritual life.

The Holy Spirit is the *"other"* advocate sent specifically to abide with us forever: *"If you love me, keep my commandments. And I will pray the Father, and He will give **another** Helper, that he may abide with you forever--even the Spirit of Truth...for he dwells with you and will be in you"* (John 14:15,16). In the original Greek the word "another" is a second helper but equal, identical, in nothing inferior but even superior in another sense. As Jesus in his bodily presence had been to his disciples, so would the Spirit be present with all believers wherever they might be or on every occasion.

In practical terms we are so much more aware of our body than of our spirit. Our spirit remains so often a virtual non entity. For the believer temptation approaches us most directly through the *"body of sin."* Paul has said in effect: *Stop presenting your members as instruments of unrighteousness to sin."* He lists the specific sins of the body and soul (Galatians 5:19-21). The sins of the mind and emotions are possibly viewed as more subtle, "less" sinful – envy, jealousy, fear, and heading the list, as always, perennial pride.

Paul challenges us to *"cleanse yourselves from all filthiness of the flesh and **spirit**, perfecting holiness in the fear of God"* (2 Corinthians 7:1). Sins of the spirit could be the often hidden attitudes of "soulishness" or fleshliness that cripple our faith and grieve the Holy Spirit. To struggle and even serve God in sincerity but in the soulish energy of the flesh is never acceptable to Holy Spirit. He can never bless such labor per se. He may bless the Word preached and in his sovereignty accomplish his own purposes, but at the Judgment Seat of Christ such ministry with be *"wood, hay, stubble"* and be consumed in a moment.

I am not dogmatic about the Biblical nature of man. God has more important truths to teach us. Two views may be given as descriptions rather than definitions. Both appeal to Scripture for support and Scripture gives some basis for both: the bipartite or tripartite understanding. The bipartite or two-fold essence of man is material and the non-material: body and soul/spirit, non-material.

I prefer without dogmatism the tripartite view with the distinctive of the spirit as the potential of God consciousness. *"That which is born of the flesh is flesh, and that which born of the Spirit is spirit"* (John 3:6). A Pauline benediction may indicate the priority: *"Now may the God of peace Himself sanctify you completely; and may your **whole spirit, soul, and body** be preserved blameless at the coming of our Lord Jesus Christ"* (1 Thessalonians 5:23; Hebrews 4:12). The three-fold description is: the spirit, the dwelling place of the divine Spirit; the soul, our emotions, mind and will; the body, being the material part with an openness to the world in which we live.

God has given to the spirit of man the highest honor of being the dwelling place of the Holy Spirit. It is true that the *"body is the temple of the Holy Spirit"* (1 Corinthians 6:19), but the tabernacle had the holy place and the Holiest of Holies. There dwelt the Ark of the Covenant and the Shekinah glory. Jesus made it clear that God is Spirit (John 4:24) and, as such, is never limited to the body. The marvel of the incarnation was that God found a way for his Son to tabernacle among us be our savior.

*"On the last day, that great day of the feast, Jesus stood and cried out, saying, 'If anyone thirst, let him come to Me and drink. He who believes in Me, as the Scripture has said, **out of his heart** will flow rivers of living water.' But this He spoke*

concerning the Spirit, whom those believing in Him would receive; for the Holy Spirit was not yet given [at Pentecost], because Christ was not yet glorified" (John 7: 37-39). Another version translates "out of his innermost being" will flow rivers of living water--the spirit.

God, the Holy Spirit, then, relates to us, to our spirit directly; the spirit in turn should regulate the life of the soul and body under Biblical orders; that is, the order ordained by God for our safety. Emotions are undependable, the body susceptible to a wide range of temptation. The Spirit filled life is then an ordered and holy life.

Another word of caution. There are dangers inherent in spirit-related experiences. There is the genuine work of the Holy Spirit always grounded in the Word. But there are demonic and psychic powers that counterfeit and deceive the believer. Great caution is needed to not open oneself to such foreign powers.

The Welsh Revival of 1905 began with remarkable true Spirit experiences. But the watch word became: "Obey the Spirit," and soon indiscriminate seeking of experiences opened the door to the demonic and psychic. A true work of God degenerated into counterfeit experiences that quenched the Spirit and ended prematurely the revival. God used the teachings of Mrs. Penn-Lewis to bring a Biblical balance by returning Evan Roberts and other leaders to the truths of Romans 6: 6. Her writings through the years have been blessed and have safeguarded thousands through the Keswick movement. I personally and my family owe much to her sane and balanced writing on our union with Christ.

She affirmed that the Holy Spirit never directly relates his ministry to the body or soul but rather to the spirit with the mind fully engaged in the Word of God. There may be the overflow of joy in blessing in our emotions with God's deeper dealings. But any true experience should return us to the Cross of Christ. To be so-called "slain in the spirit," or "tumbado" (Spanish for "knocked down") becomes extremely dangerous and unbiblical.

What, then, is our motivation to be? I remember the light that dawned on my heart in Prairie Bible Institute when I read Andrew Murray's *"The Spirit of Christ."* is sane advice was: We must know him as a person, venerate his solemn work in us and relate to him as we do to the other members of the Divine Trinity. Such a conscious sensitivity to his spiritual presence is a process but comes with obedience to the Word of God as illuminated to us by the Spirit himself.

Chapter 27

REIGNING WITH CHRIST IN SUFFERING

Romans 8:17, 18

We don't ordinarily associate being the adopted sons of God and therefore *"heirs--heirs of God and joint heirs with Christ"* with those who are also destined to suffer. Such a thought appears at first thought to be incongruent; it does not seem to follow. However, that is precisely what Paul says as he introduces this paragraph. *"The Spirit Himself bears witness with our spirit that we are children of God, and if children, then heirs--of God and joint heirs with Christ, **if indeed we suffer with Him**, that we may also be glorified together"* (Romans 8:16,17).

Remember that Paul is tracing the marks and characteristics of the victorious believer. After the new point of departure of *"but if **by the Spirit** you put to death the deeds of the body, you will live"* (v.13), Paul immediately states the first blessing: *"For as many as are led by the Spirit of God, these are the sons of God."* He follows it up by our receiving the Spirit of adoption by which we cry out: "Abba, Father."

These verses, then, are a closely knit pattern of truths. We cannot expect the blessings without also receiving from the same gracious hand the sufferings that sons must undergo. God's own son suffered in our behalf. Can we object to joining him in his suffering?

The Enigma of Suffering in Romans 8

The ultimate puzzle that has challenged mankind has always been the "why" of suffering. In the chapter devoted most fully to victory in a Risen Christ, suffering is an integral part of the victorious life to be lived. Paul in his last epistle and challenge to Timothy has summed up what was a common Christian refrain: *"This is a faithful saying: For if we died with Him, we shall also live with Him.* ***If we endure, we shall also reign with Him****. If we deny Him, He also will deny us. If we are faithless, He remains faithful: He cannot deny Himself"* (2 Timothy 2:11-13).

God does not ever answer our questions of "why" when grounded in our anxiety and shortsightedness. He responds by showing us himself and the ultimate issue that eternity will reveal. If there was one who suffered and finally came to understand, it was Job. He cut the Gordian knot; he lived out God's principle of death to self. Our mission is submission.

God introduces Job as blameless and upright who shunned iniquity. God in silence allowed the fiery furnace of the enemy's attack, the false judgments of well-meaning friends and the wiser counsel of Elihu. Job responds in confident self-defense but finally he runs out of words.

Finally God speaks: *"Who is this who darkens counsel by words without knowledge? Now prepare yourself like a man; I will question you, and you shall answer Me"* (Job. 38:2, 3). Then later out of a whirlwind God repeats: *"Now prepare yourself like a man; I will question you, and you shall answer Me: Would you indeed annul My judgment? Would you condemn Me that you may be justified?* (Job. 40:7.8). What a direct blow to Job's self-righteousness!

God will ask Job a total of 80 questions from the physical world (Job 38-41). Job is not able to answer even one, let alone understand the spiritual truths. He is devastated, undone and broken by suffering. But he now knows more importantly who God is and who he is not: "*I have heard of You by the hearing of the ear, but now my eyes sees You. Therefore I abhor myself, and repent in dust and ashes*" (Job 42:5, 6).

God never answered one of his questions, but through suffering he broke the core of Job's self-righteousness. In New Testament language Job died to his self-life. In doing so God revealed himself and the spiritual pride of Job. God's deeper dealing through suffering led to Job's transformation and double blessing. Job is the Old Testament commentary on suffering as the New Testament reveals the suffering of God himself and his beloved Son in our behalf.

The Greatest of Mysteries-The Triune God Who Suffered Most

The Cross revealed God's infinite holiness and love beyond compare. A simple question: Who has suffered the most? Although we swim in uncharted waters, the answer is clear. The Triune God himself suffered infinitely more than we could ever grasp or imagine. In the eternal counsels of the Triune God, the Father sent his Son to die and the Holy Spirit would raise him from the dead.

Here our theology is easily stated, but the depths of that involvement will forever be the theme and the song of eternity. "*Worthy is the Lamb who was slain to receive power and riches and wisdom, and strength and honor and glory and blessing! . . . Blessing and honor and glory and power be to*

Him who sits on the throne, and to the Lamb forever and ever!" (Revelation 5:12, 13).

The Bible gives a chain of references to the Triune God in those ages past: "*He indeed was foreordained before the foundation of the world, but was manifest in these last times for you*" (1 Peter 1:20). With reference to the tribulation: "*And all who dwell on the earth will worship him* [the antichrist] *whose names have not been written in the Book of life of the Lamb slain from the foundation of the world*" (Revelation 13:8). In Peter's inaugural message at Pentecost he expressed God's eternal plan: "*Him being delivered by the **determined counsel and foreknowledge of God,** you have taken by lawless hands, have crucified and put to death; whom God has raised up...*" (Acts 2:23, 24).

But the verses that resonate eternally, impossible for us to grasp are: "*A Man of sorrows and acquainted with grief . . . Surely He has borne our griefs and carried our sorrows; yet we esteemed Him stricken, **smitten by God and afflicted**. But he was wounded for our transgressions, He was bruised for our iniquities . . . **Yet it pleased the LORD to bruise Him;** He has put Him to grief. When You make His soul an offering for sin, He shall see His seed, He shall prolong His days and the pleasure of the LORD shall prosper in His hand*" (Isaiah 53:3, 4, 5, 10). Yet it was this very God who, with his Son's full consent, would bruise him, "*the just for the unjust that he might bring us to God*" (1 Peter 3:18).

Only through God's infinite suffering can we begin to know God, his righteousness in exacting death from his own Son and in priceless love paying the price himself for "bruising" his own Son" for us. On the other hand, "*about the ninth hour Jesus cried out with a loud voice, saying, 'Eli, Eli, lama sabachthani?'*

that is, 'My God, My God, why have You forsaken Me?'" (Matthew 27:46).

These are depths that we cannot fathom. "*In the days of his flesh, when he had offered up prayers and supplications with vehement cries and tears to Him who was able to save him from death, and was heard because of his godly fear*" (Hebrews 5:7). If the Son of God suffered so, should we not expect as the sons of God to accept our spiritual heritage?

If the Son of God, unique in his deity and **humanity,** suffered for us, should not we cherish the honor of sharing in his sufferings! Paul expressed it precisely as the overwhelming passion of his life: "*That I may know Him and the power of His resurrection, and the fellowship* ["koinonía"--partnership] *of his sufferings, being conformed to His death*" (Philippians 3:10).

Suffering-an Extension of the Fall of Man

There can be no question but suffering is a direct result of the fall, man's yielding to Satan in the Garden of Eden. The immediate pronouncement of the curse was to the woman: "*I will greatly multiply your sorrow and your conception....Then to Adam he said, Cursed is the ground for your sake; in toil you shall eat of it all the days of your life . . . for dust you are, and to dust you shall return*" (Genesis 3:16, 17, 19).

When the believer suffers because of his own sin, God has nothing to do with it; "*Do not be deceived, God is not mocked; for whatever a man sows, that he will also reap. For he who sows to his flesh will of the flesh reap corruption, but he who sows to the Spirit will of the Spirit reap everlasting life*" (Galatians 6:7, 8). However, if the believer repents and turns in brokenness and contrition, the blood of Christ will cleanse from all sin. God may even mitigate some of the consequences of the sin. Consequences will, however, inevitably follow. Such occasions and lessons learned can serve for future caution and profit.

Suffering in the Life of the Believer

In no way has God granted an exemption to the believer from the reality of our sinful world. The Christian is subject to death at any age, natural disasters, cancer and the widest range of human congenital defects. However, even these can become God's **providential sufferings** and to them he adds his grace and strength.

I suffered life-threatening polio at sixteen and a diagnosed throat cancer that threatened the future use of my voice; our granddaughter had leukemia which God healed and later she suffered a cavernoma (brain hemorrhage) which God is healing and our grandson was born with cystic fibrosis. But God has turned each of these **providential sufferings** into deeper lessons learned by all of us. Our text says: *"if indeed we suffer with Him that we may also be glorified together."* These very tribulations become our investment in future glory. What a different perspective that gives to us, even in the midst of human anguish and sorrow!

If we accept by faith that he oversees our **providential sufferings** and we turn to him in submission and obedience, these become an integral part of our present transformation and our future reward. As divine suffering revealed the gracious nature of God to a lost world, so providential sufferings reveal our weakness but in our weakness we can draw on his strength and others upon seeing God's grace in us give him glory.

The Essence of Christ's Suffering—Our Service in Union with Him

Paul has much to say, however, about another kind of suffering, **suffering for the gospel's sake** in obedience to his will. These are the true sufferings of the believer that produce the very life of Christ in us. Paul has dedicated a whole epistle, 2 Corinthians, to exalt the true sufferings of the apostle for Christ's sake.

Paul begins the epistle with overflowing praise. *"Blessed be the God and Father of our Lord Jesus Christ, the Father of mercies and God of all comfort* [encouragement]*, who comforts us in all our tribulation, that we may be able to comfort those who are in any trouble with the comfort with which we ourselves are comforted by God. For as the sufferings of Christ abound in us, so our consolation also abounds through Christ"* (2 Corinthians 1:3-5).

He develops this theme in the full duress of Christian service. He ministers in the power of the risen Christ. *"For we do not want you to be ignorant, brethren, of our trouble which came to us in Asia; that we were burdened beyond measure, above strength, so that we despaired even of life. Yes, we had the* **sentence of death in ourselves**, *that we should not trust in ourselves, but in God who raises the dead, who delivers us from so great a death, and does deliver us; in whom we trust that He will still deliver us"* (2 Corinthians 1: 9-10).

Suffering in obedience to the will of God for Christ's sake becomes a doorway of hope. Again, Paul says: *"But we have this treasure in earthen vessels, that the excellence of the power may be of God, and not of us. We are hard pressed on every side, yet not crushed; we are perplexed, but not in* despair; persecuted, but not forsaken; struck down, but not destroyed—always carrying about in the body the dying of the Lord Jesus, that the life of Jesus also may be manifested in our body" (4:7-10).

Paul thus describes the crucified life, hid with Christ in God. Suffering, then, is our badge of honor. Death (to self) works in us that Christ's risen life may spring up in others (4:12). This is the true dynamic of Christian service, so often overlooked. What so often follows is our dependency on intellectualism, head theology, education and seminary degrees, natural talent and soulish energy—all poor substitutes for the risen life of Christ springing from the Cross. Human efforts can only produce human results; Christ's resurrection life produces lasting and abiding fruit.

What follows is God's dynamic. Paul has strikingly presented the greater glory of the Spirit's ministration: "*Now the Lord is the Spirit: and where the Spirit of the Lord is, there is liberty. But we all, with unveiled face, beholding as in a mirror the glory of the Lord, are being transformed into the same image from glory to glory, just as by the Spirit of the Lord. Therefore, since we have this ministry, as we have received mercy we do not lose heart. But we have renounced the hidden things of shame, not walking in craftiness nor handling the word of God deceitfully, but by manifestation of the truth commending ourselves to everyman's conscience in the sight of God*" (2 Corinthians 3:17-4:2).

As adopted sons, heirs of God and joint heirs with Christ, ours is the privilege to see God turn our sufferings into the gold of his glory.

Across the will of nature leads on the path of God;
Not where the flesh delighteth the feet of Jesus trod.
Oh, bliss to leave behind us the fetters of the slave,
To leave **ourselves** behind us, the grave-clothes
and the grave!

Gerhard Ter Steegen,
(1697-1759)

Chapter 28

NEW HORIZONS OF THE SPIRIT'S WORK

Romans 8:19-27

Paul turns from suffering to the glorious future that awaits the sons of God. He looks backward and then projects forward to the future consummation of the Work of the Cross. Such future certainties challenge our understanding of the majesty of his grace.

In other epistles Paul glimpses what is to come. In Romans he outlines it in broad strokes of its glory. He frames the future in terms of **Hope.** It is not, however, the hope of human wishful thinking, but in the sovereign surety of God's plan destined to unfold to God's greater glory.

Paul often strikes the comparison of the present with the glorious future. *"For I consider that the sufferings of this present time are not worthy to be compared with the glory which shall be revealed in us"* (8:19). This is Paul's considered judgment reflected also in his theme of suffering and glory in 2 Corinthians. *"For our light affliction, which is but for a moment, is working for us a far more exceeding and eternal weight of glory, while we do not look at things which are seen, but at things which are not seen. For the things which are seen* are temporary, but the things which are not seen are eternal" (2 Corinthians 4: 17, 18). As in life so in the spiritual realm-- perspective is only gained by the long range view.

Paul's Abiding Hope and Expectation   Romans 8:19-25

What is most obvious is that Paul's projected look is the **expectation of the future**. The future is wisely hidden from our eyes. Faith, not sight, is our north star. But God operates on the long range view. In ways that we cannot appreciate, God is preparing yet more wonderful days ahead. Paul quotes the open-ended prophecy: *"But it is written: Eye has not seen, nor ear heard, nor have entered into the heart of man the things which God has prepared for those who love Him"* (1 Corinthians 2:9; Isaiah 64:4; 65:17). Verse 10 states, however: "But God has revealed them to us through His Spirit."

The Spirit does reveal the short term wonders but much more awaits God's time table. It is not given to us to understand in depth the breadth of God's redemption, but Paul does infer that the original divine creation will yet have its own glorious future grounded in the ultimate investiture of the sons of God (v.19).

The entrance of sin into the Garden of Eden was not only the fall of man, but creation itself fell through no fault of its own; it reaped the repercussions of the man's rebellion. In fact, the first words of condemnation of God to Adam were: *"Cursed is the ground for your sake . . . both thorns and thistles it shall bring forth for you"* (Genesis 3:17, 18). Creation itself was unwillingly involved in Adam's guilt.

It may surprise us but all of God's original creation fell under his love: the moral and human and also the physical. God had an eternal plan beyond man's redemption, a full redemption for his physical creation. *"Because the creation itself also will be delivered from the bondage of corruption into the glorious liberty of the children of God"* (v.21). That "earnest expectation" will be triggered by the fullness of his son's redemption.

Paul introduces now the abiding concept of hope. God has a divine triad; faith, hope and love. While the greatest of the three is love (1 Corinthians 13:13), faith is the ruling principle of the present and hope is the ruling principle of the future. Love has always been the eternally governing principle of God's sovereign plan.

In this paragraph Paul speaks of the "earnest expectation" and six times refers to hope and twice to our waiting for the fulfillment of God's eternal plan. Paul is anticipating John's statement: *"And I saw a new heaven and a new earth, for the first heaven and the first earth had passed away. Also there was no more sea . . . Then He who sat upon the throne said: 'Behold I make all things new'"* (Revelation 21:1, 5).

Paul draws on the wholeness of God's creation, a fact we seldom grasp in its entirety. Under the crushing rule of sin, both creations *"groan and labor with birth pains together until now"* (v.22). But Paul returns to his assurance of hope. God defines hope very differently than we do. Our hope is often an aspiration, a possible "winning of the Power lottery." God's hope is the unfolding on his timetable--everything based firmly on the accomplishments wrought once for all at the Cross. Because God deals in the triumph of the past, the Cross of Christ, hope is not a postponement but an event sure to happen.

Faith is, first of all, a divine-human reaction to the integrity of God's Word and Spirit. It is a non- meritorious element on our part. Hope, on the other hand, rests solely on God's gracious timetable and promise. *"But if we hope for what we do not see, then we eagerly wait for it with perseverance"* (v.25).

The Gracious Prayer Ministry of the Holy Spirit
Romans 8:26, 27

At first reading it may seem to us that Paul is introducing a totally different topic, the ministry of prayer. In fact, this is the first time in the body of Romans that he speaks of prayer. Is it a strange omission? I think not. In the later part of Romans, he will make many practical applications of the truths of Romans 5-8, so foundational to life and ministry (cf., Romans 12:12).

It is crucial that we note the first word: **"*Likewise* the Spirit *also* helps in our weaknesses. For we do not know what to pray for as we ought . . ."** (v. 26). The two words "likewise" and "also" tie the Spirit's prayer ministry directly into the immediate context. Just as we do not know and cannot foresee the coming redemption of the creation and the sons of God, so also in the ministry of prayer, we do not know what to ask for. The Spirit helps our infirmities as we walk by faith and yet are filled with hope.

It may appear strange that prayer in Romans is not given a higher priority. But Romans is a powerful presentation of the truths of the Cross; what God did and offers to us in grace is to be received by faith and thanksgiving. Too often our concept of prayer is the request of beggar: "Gimme," help me to be more holy, more like Christ, more humble, ad infinitum.

Dr. F. J. Huegel used to say: "Praise or thanksgiving is faith in full bloom." With the "divine help" of the Spirit, based exclusively on God's judgment of our sin at the Cross, victory in union with Christ is ours for the taking and receiving without fasting or effort, or much less, merit.

The Majestic Development of Romans 8

Romans 8 is the highlight of the fullness of the Holy Spirit available to the believer. Paul mentions the Spirit some 21 times in 39 verses. Previously he had made only two earlier references to him. (5:5 and 7:6). Romans 8 is like a skyscraper. Its height depends on its firm foundation.

Paul had established salvation's foundation in justification, solidarity with the Last Adam, our union with Christ in death to sin and risen in his resurrection. Now he assumes the walk according to the Spirit, the believer's new point of departure: *"but if **by the Spirit** you put to death the deeds of the body, you will live"* (8:13).

Now comes the list of blessings: guidance, the Spirit of adoption, the witness of the Spirit, heirs and joint heir and suffering that ends in glory. In the midst of "groanings" the Spirit brings hope. In prayer God searches the heart and the Spirit who knows the will of God helps our infirmities. What a chain of blessings, all proceeding from the Holy Spirit!

So often the believer fails to realize his resources in prayer. Hebrews reveals the intercession of Christ, our High Priest, in our behalf. What powerful and immediate access to the throne! *"Therefore He is also able to save to the uttermost those who come to God through Him, since He ever lives to make intercession for them"* (Hebrews 7:25). Added to Christ's effective intercession is another's: *"But the Spirit Himself makes intercession for us with groanings which cannot be uttered"* (v.26).

Chapter 28: New horizons of the Spirit's work

A Side Note--the Ministry of the Holy Spirit in the Old Testament

The currently popular interpretation is that the Holy Spirit did not indwell the Old Testament saint, but rather came and went as attested in the time of the Judges and Prophets. By contrast after the Cross the believer is now indwelt and sealed. The two salvations are contrasted or compared, one better than the other. There is a partial truth in the above position, but it is flawed in its comparison of the Old with the New.

The position of the New Testament saint is most correctly presented as indwelt by the Holy Spirit from the very moment of conversion or salvation. However, to compare the saints in the two Testaments, one before the Cross and one after the Cross is to do a disservice to the Old Testament and its saints: Enoch, Joseph, Abraham, Daniel and many more.

There are some major differences between to the two testaments. Before the Cross God chose to work through the seed of Abraham and the believing Jewish people, chosen with a view to provide for the incarnation of Christ according to OT prophecies. Israel, because of its unbelief, would be set aside **temporarily** for the introduction of a new vehicle, the Church, the Body of Christ, both Jews and Gentiles. The baptism of the Spirit would inaugurate the Church as God's arm of reaching the world in this dispensation. The Jewish believing remnant will be re-instated in the future millennial Kingdom of God (Romans 11:12, 25-27).

It is too much to expect that both Testaments would use the identical terminology. The Cross with the incarnation and Christ's vicarious death marks off human history. His resurrection could not be stated historically in the Old Testament. However, we know that in God's plan Christ died from before the foundation of the world; we were chosen by God from eternity past in the mind and plan of God (Ephesians 1:4, 5; 1 Peter 2:19, 20; Revelation 13:8).

Therefore, the virtues of his death were as available to the saint of the Old Testament in their *personal salvation before God* on the basis of grace and faith as to the saints of the New (Ephesians 2: 8, 9). They in faith believed in the One who was to come just as we have believed in the One who came and died. Our position is much clearer historically than theirs, but theirs is nonetheless no less genuine. See Hebrew 11, the gallery of faith heroes.

In Genesis 15:6 we read, *"And he believed in the LORD and He accounted it to him for righteousness."* Paul quotes the identical verse in Romans 4:3. Jesus before the Cross spoke to Nicodemus of the new birth or regeneration and was surprised that he did not know (John 3:1-15). Abraham is the father of faith and we are his seed (Galatians 3:29).

I cannot conceive of two salvations, one better, the other inferior. What is *explicit* in the New Testament was *implicit* in the Old. The spirituality of the saints of the Old (Hebrews 11) equals the saints of the New. The Eternal Spirit operated through faith and grace in both Testaments. Christ is hidden or latent in the Old Testament and revealed or patent in the New.

This position is fully developed by Dr. Leon J. Wood, a Ph.D in Hebrew and Baptist professor, in his book: *The Holy Spirit in the Old Testament*.

Chapter 29

THE MAJESTY OF GOD'S ETERNAL PLAN

Romans 8:28-34

Paul will be our guide as we climb Mount Everest, God's majestic ascent, as set forth in this glorious chapter. Dr. F. J. Huegel, often referred to Romans 8 as the Christian Mount Everest. The Sherpa guide who led Sir Edmond Hilary to the top of Everest on May 19, 1953 well knew that the ascent was a series of plateaus to be conquered before setting the flag on the pinnacle. In our study in Romans we are ascending the plateaus that will culminate in the triumphant eternal entrance into his presence.

All too often isolated texts from Romans 8 have been taken and applied to the Christian life independently of the context without real spiritual success. But Romans 5-8 is a series of plateaus that the Spirit makes possible based on our response in obedience to the walk of faith. We cannot appropriate the blessings of Romans 8 while walking according to the flesh and ignoring the truths of the preceding chapters.

Recently I was guiding a student through her faith walk in Romans 5-8. She confessed to me that she had been living in personal spiritual defeat, even though serving God on her student assignments. Her solution was to memorize Romans 8. During the summer she frequently repeated it, but nothing changed. Now we were sharing our solidarity with the Second Adam in chapter 5, our death to sin and identification with

Christ and the steps of the faith-walk in 6, our spiritual marriage or union with Christ and ceasing from our own struggles under law in 7 and the fullness of Spirit in 8. Now she had entered in and commented voluntarily: "Now I know why nothing changed. I knew nothing of the preceding chapters."

The Christian Life Stated in Romans 8:28

The first rule of Biblical interpretation is to consider carefully the influence of the context. It has been often said: the text without its context is a pretext. Paul has been presenting the daily faith walk of the believer according to the Spirit in Romans 8:1-13.Verse 13 is the fulcrum, the pivot that results in the blessings of the rest of the chapter.

We cannot omit: *"For if you live according to the flesh you will die* [not a practical option in the light of the context]*; but if by the Spirit you put to death the deeds of the flesh, you will live* [the evident option]." With the walk after the Spirit now a faith reality, the believer will experience the following blessings, as cause is to effect.

From Romans 8:18-27 Paul has been developing the role of **Hope** from the "groaning" of creation to the "groanings" of the believer; we await the adoption of sons. God's definition of hope is a future certainty. The new creation will burst forth in his time. We anticipate that specific time but cannot grasp its full meaning. But we believe it and **Faith** becomes knowing. Remember chapter 8 is devoted to the diverse ministries of the Holy Spirit: *"Now He who searches the heart knows what the mind of the Spirit is, because He makes intercession of the saints according to the will of God"* (v.27). The issue is: God knows fully what he is doing and the Spirit is his agent to accomplish it in the believer.

Notice now how tightly Paul weaves the knowledge of God and his purposes into the verse so often quoted without a context. With that in mind Paul says in effect: and *we know and that to the **ones loving God,** all things work together for good, to those according to purpose being called*" [v.28--literal translation]. This is the syntax or word order that expresses Paul's strong emphasis.

Paul is saying: we may not know the fullness of the future, but the Spirit now makes known to the believer **who loves God** that, indeed all, everything, is working together for his good as God knows what is good. Notice the emphasis given to those loving God. The emphasis and importance of loving God are not as evident in the English text. What an assurance that God is in control and by **faith we know** with certainty that God is actively working out his likeness in us! This knowledge is a step of faith.

> Nothing before, nothing behind; the steps of faith
> Fall on the seeming void, and find the rock beneath.

J. G. Whittier

Earlier in the chapter Paul has developed the divine triad of **Faith, Hope** and now **Love.** God makes everything work together for good to those who respond to his **Love** (1 John 4:19). We observed earlier that Faith is the governing principle of the present, Hope the governing principle of the future and Love his governing principle of eternity.

The verse does not say categorically in the abstract that everything that happens to the believer is good. Sickness, bankruptcy, death of a child, natural catastrophe, often the consequences of natural evil are not good. There is what is bad and troubling, but under that divine control God can make them work together for our ultimate good, our *summum bonum* (our highest good).

In one sense Romans 5:3-5 anticipates what God will prove in the later chapters; *"And not only that... but tribulation produces perseverance; and perseverance, character; and character, hope. Now hope does not disappoint because the **love of God** has been poured out in our hearts by the **Holy Spirit** who was given to us."* Romans 8:28 restates it as an established reality. Faith, Hope and Love have come together to bless the believer in every possible circumstance of life.

God's Ultimate Good for the Believer--Conformed to the Image of His Son   Romans 8:28

Another plateau is before us. Paul now proceeds to introduce us to the inscrutable ways of God. We are much concerned about what may occur in our lives: the blessings of health, family and even Christian service. But these are all, in the last analysis, secondary to God highest purpose. God has a far greater blessing to bestow. He initiated a calling, an effective calling in grace and mercy. It was totally of his doing. No chain is stronger than its weakest link. No effort or merit of ours could ever have been a single link in God's chain.

Whomever he calls responds freely and voluntarily. This statement may seem like a denial of the God-given will and choice of the believer, but here we bow in submission to God's ways *"being past finding out."* With good reason Paul concludes the major section of Romans with this paean of praise: *"Oh, the depths of the riches both of the wisdom and* *knowledge of God! How unsearchable are His judgments and **His ways past finding out!**"* (Romans 11: 33).

We do not seek an intellectual explanation. Our own genuine experience with God, as best we can understand it, testifies to the fact we were never coerced in order to believe. We did not seek him, but he sought us. Our response was never as immediate as it should have been nor of our initiative. We were moved by our desperate needs as we had never seen them before; we were moved by his mercy and grace.

Called...Foreknown...Predestined...To Be Conformed
Romans 8:29

Throughout this whole passage in Romans, the divine initiative is highlighted. Our salvation is stated in the passive voice what God has done for us and in us; the indicative mood of reality establishes the historical authenticity of what God did at the cross, a once for all event with eternal consequences.

God's foreknowledge, as difficult as it may be for us to understand, was never dependent on what we would do. God took care of that: *"Just as He chose us in Him, before the foundation of the world, that **we should be holy and without blame before Him in love**"* (Ephesians 1:4). The fact that he chose us before we were ever conceived eliminates any merit or contribution. Furthermore he chose us *in love.* How can we object to being the object of his love?

Paul takes note that God has not provided a mere passport to heaven nor a panacea to guarantee riches or wealth. Unfortunately today there are "theologies" that cater to man's material and social needs. Prosperity Theology has birthed mega-churches whose standards are man-centered.

But God paid the highest price possible, the death of his own son. He will be satisfied with nothing less than a conversion that results in a transformed life.

The Bible makes it crystal clear that personal holiness alone pleases God. *Do you not know that the unrighteous will not inherit the kingdom of God? Do not be deceived. Neither fornicators, nor idolaters, nor adulterers, nor homosexuals, nor sodomites, nor thieves, nor covetous, nor drunkards, nor revilers, nor extortioners will inherit the kingdom of God. And such were some of you. But you were washed, but you were sanctified, but you were justified in the name of the Lord Jesus and by the Spirit of our God"* (1 Corinthians 6:9-11). Writing to the Corinthian Christians who were living in a city that was world famous for licentious lifestyle, Paul commends their transformation, an inward work of grace.

God purposes no less than to make his firstborn Son the model among many brethren. God said of his own Son at baptism and transfiguration: *"This is My beloved Son, in whom I am well pleased"* (Matthew 3:17; Luke 9:35). Every provision has been made for the indwelling Christ to be the very life of the believer. Romans has been the handbook, the manual of that process that God launched before the foundation of the world. He is committed to nothing less.

Four Decrees of Grace: Predestined...Called...Justified... Glorified   Romans 8:30

What follows is the climax of Paul's argument that began with condemnation and ends in glorification. In four terse statements, all in the aorist or past tense, God sums up what in grace he did. There is no equivocation. From eternity past God had sent his son to die vicariously for man and so magnify his righteousness, love and his grace. God's **Grand Design** would redound ultimately *"to the praise of the glory of his grace,"* the repetitive theme of the doxology (Ephesians 1:6a, 12, 14).

What follows is the **Grand Design**, the eternal chain of God's gracious initiative. The four links in the chain would each be grounded in God's righteous decree and the work of the Cross of Christ. Nothing can be added to or removed from the finality and efficacy of the death and resurrection of Jesus Christ.

The initial work of God is the **election** or his marking out beforehand the choice of adopted sons, a work of sovereign grace. Here we tread on sacred ground that we are called to accept and not deny. God's truth transcends our limited knowledge of God. But in faith we accept God's truth. Ephesians begins with the doxology of the **Grand Design**.

*"Blessed be the God and Father of our Lord Jesus Christ, who has blessed us with every spiritual blessing in the heavenly places in Christ, just as he **chose us in Him** before the foundation of the world, that we should be holy and without blame before Him in love, **having predestined us to adoption** as sons of Jesus Christ to Himself according to the good pleasure of His will, to the praise of the glory of His grace"* (Ephesians 1:3-6).

The second link in the chain is his effective **calling.** God chose us in Him before the foundation of the world; no one, therefore, could claim a scintilla of merit or worth. God does not reveal to our curiosity on what basis he chose us. The Ephesian doxology make it clear that he blessed us and chose us to be holy and without blame before him **in love,** having predestined us to adoption. What follows is his matchless seeking of the sinner, his wooing of the wicked. He sought us; we did not seek him.

If someone objects to God's effective calling, let him hear God's plea. *"Ho! Everyone who thirsts, come to the waters; and you who have no money, come, buy and eat. Yes, come, buy wine and milk . . . Listen diligently to Me, and eat what is good, and let your soul delight itself in abundance"* (Isaiah 55:1,2). The New Testament version is: *"On the last day, the great day of the feast, Jesus stood and cried out saying, 'If any man thirst, let him come to Me and drink as the Scripture has said, out of his heart will flow rivers of living water'"* (John 7:37,38).

It is important to observe the timing of the introduction of the Biblical doctrine of God's election and calling. It is introduced in the very last verses of Romans 8 as **a doctrine for the family of God** who have been wooed and won by God's grace and mercy. God changes the heart and then shares his love and blessing on our mind and will.

The third link is **justified.** Paul has devoted 64 verses to man's depravity (Romans 1:18-3:20) and then follows that with 47 verses (3:21-4:25) devoted to how God the righteous Judge could forgive the ungodly. A description of justification may be: the divine decree of the Just Judge who **declares** the ungodly who believes as righteous as his own Son on the basis of his vicarious death by which God forgives the ungodly and restores him to the full range of privileges of an adopted son of God. As such, his ruling is eternal, secure and inviolate. The believer has a new and firm standing before God.

One may ask why is sanctification not included? The four links in the chain are exclusively the work of God, totally apart from man's merit or effort. Remember true faith carries no merit whatsoever. Faith can only receive what God offers. Sanctification is the fruit or evidence of justification and as such is included in God's concept of justification. One other reason may be that in the believer, holiness is an ongoing moral work of God's grace, a process rather than an accomplishment.

The fourth and final link is **glorification.** While future to our time frame, it is as firm and final as the other links. The Ephesian doxology states: *"You were sealed with the Holy Spirit of promise, who is the guarantee of our inheritance until the redemption of the purchased possession, **to the praise of his glory**"* (Ephesians 1:14).

Chapter 30

CONSUMMATION AND CONFIDENCE IN CHRST

Romans 8:31-39

We come to the consummation and confidence of the Message of the Cross as lived out in the life of the believer who walks here and now by faith. What a journey of grace and divine mercy! The sinner's life began with separation, rebellion and final **condemnation** (Romans 1:18-3:20), but all was not lost because of the sheer mercy and love of God who found a righteous way to **declare the ungodly just** -- through the vicarious death of his own Son who took the sinner's place and paid the price of his redemption (3:21-4:25).

But after dealing effectively with the sins of believer, God dealt with the *sin principle* in the believer by uniting him to **Christ who "died once for all to sin"** (5:1-8:13). **In that judicial death we died and now are united to Christ; we share his risen life in the power of the Holy Spirit.** Holiness or sanctification then becomes ours as a gift of grace equally as was our justification. Both come to us through his death for us and our death in him.

The believer now shares the risen life of Christ by the presence and enablement of the Holy Spirit. His enablement ours by faith, not by struggle or effort. **It is not imitation of Christ but by participation in his life, made ours on a moment**

by moment basis of trust and commitment. Paul unveils the reality of life in union with Christ (Romans 8:14-30).

Paul sets the believer in Christ squarely in God's **Grand Design** of eternity; the believer lives in vital union with him, walking by faith in heart obedience. There is divine purpose, direction, enablement and fulfillment. Everything that touches the believer is a part of God's master plan to conform us to the image of his Son, he being *"the firstborn of many brethren."* This eliminates the "why" or "what" of doubt and gives to us the rest of faith. All of God's purposes are being fulfilled and we are the beneficiaries. We see God's commitment to holiness in heart and life. Nothing more or less.

Five Resonating Questions that Silence Forever Any Enemy
Romans 8:31-35

As is customary, Paul introduces new truths and applications with brief questions, such as: "What then . . .?" (Romans 3:1, 9; 4:1; 6:1, 15; 7:7). In this way he signals the next plateau in the believer's climb. Now for the last time with a triumphant note of expectation: *"What then shall we say to these things? If God be for us, who can be against us?"* (v.31). The first question is a rhetorical one that really needs no answer. He argues: If or since there is no one greater than God and he has shown himself to be for us in the sending his own Son, who under the sun could stand in his way of completing his work of grace? Paul's logic is convincing indeed.

Immediately such a question brings to mind the crisis at Kadesh Barnea with the response of the ten spies who saw only the giants and walled cities and said: "We can't enter." As opposed to the physical realities of the land, Caleb saw the

Lord. *"Then Caleb quieted the people before Moses, and said, 'Let us go up at once and take possession, for we are well able to overcome it.'"*

After the people's full night of wailing in unbelief, Joshua and Caleb reiterated their confidence in Jehovah: *"The land we passed through to spy out is an exceedingly good land. **If the Lord delights in us**, then He will bring us into his land and give it to us, a land which flows with milk and honey. Only do not rebel against the LORD, nor fear the people of the land, **for they are our bread**; their protection has departed from them, and LORD is with us. Do not fear them"* (Numbers 13:30; 14:8, 9).

The second rhetorical question adds yet greater proof of God's overwhelming presence (v.32). Paul adds the supreme gift of God's son in our behalf. To this gracious reality from eternity past there can be no questioning of God's favor. *"He who did not spare His own Son, but delivered Him up for us all, how shall He not with Him freely give us all things?"* (v.32) Seven hundred years earlier Isaiah broached this stupendous truth: *"Yet it pleased the Lord to bruise Him; He has put Him to grief. When You make His soul an offering for sin, He shall see His seed, He shall prolong His days, and the pleasure of the LORD shall prosper in His hand"* (Isaiah 53: 10).

The third question is terse and direct (v.33). *"Who shall bring a charge against God's elect? It is God who justifies."* Paul asserts the protection granted to the elect or those whom he called. God also knows that the walk of the believer often leaves much to be desired. Our conscience and, above all, the Devil, our adversary, does accuse us and with valid reason. But God has sheltered us against all legal condemnation. The righteous Judge has issued his final decree of the righteousness of his own Son, now our effective righteousness. This decree cannot be appealed much less challenged.

It is said of Martin Luther, one often given to self-condemnation, that when the enemy assailed him because of his sins, he seized a tablet and wrote: "The blood of Jesus Christ, God's Son, cleanses from all sin."

The fourth rhetorical question raises again the reality of our sin (v. 34). But once again the believer has a defense counselor that is impeachable. Not only does the believer have a legal and eternal standing before the Just Judge, but he also has an advocate who stands ready and able to plead the efficacy of the blood of Christ. For what more can the believer ask? *"Who is he who condemns? It is Christ who died, and furthermore is also risen, who is even at the right hand of God, who makes intercession for us."*

Hebrews develops more fully the intercessory ministry of Christ (Hebrews 1:3; 7:24, 25; 10:19-23). However, this is the first time Paul specifically connects the resurrection with the presence of Christ as our intercessor. In the mouth of two or three witnesses every word is established. The truth that Christ sits at the Father's right hand, a symbol of equality and access, lends weight to the efficacy of his prayers. We need never fear our standing before God, rather we are **"accepted in the Beloved,"** a truly unique acceptance (Ephesians 1:6).

The fifth and final question affirms no separation from the love of Christ. What greater guarantee could we ever have of security and his abiding presence! Romans 8:1 began with: *"There is therefore now no* [no kind of] *condemnation"* and the final question ends with no separation ever. *"Who shall separate us from the love Christ?"* (v.35).

These five questions and answers immediately given and supported by abiding truths afford the believer with absolute confidence to walk in faith in the indwelling Christ. Generally a rhetorical question is already so proven that no further proof is ever needed. But with Paul he has given us an overload of superlative truths to prevent the slightest doubt.

This last question begins with "who" because Paul is going to give the widest range of an imaginative flight that includes angelic beings and *"any other created being."* No one can stand in the presence of a risen Christ and defy the bonds of love that hold us. I find it interesting that the final question is centered on the **LOVE** of Christ. Ultimately God is light but he is also preeminently love. Who can question and doubt the love of another, much less the one who loved us supremely!

The Apostle John put it precisely: *"Now before the feast of the Passover, when Jesus knew that His hour had come that He should depart from this world to the Father, having loved His own who were in the world, **He loved them to the end"*** (John 13:1).

The Love of Christ Wider Than the Widest Range of Eventualities Romans   8:35-39

The final rhetorical question was asked: *"Who shall separate us from the love of Christ?"* What strikes me is our dynamic relationship with our *"Elder Brother* "(Hebrews 2:9-12), *"that he might be the firstborn among many brethren"* (v. 29). Now we see and can appreciate the wonder and mystery of the incarnation. Only the Love of the Triune God could have foreseen the unique privilege that the *"ungodly who believed"* would have, nothing less than an *"heir of God and joint heir with Christ."*

What follows is almost too sacred to comment on. *"Shall tribulation, or distress, or persecution, or famine, or nakedness, or peril, or sword? As it is written: 'For your sake we are killed all day long; We are accounted as sheep for the slaughter"* (Psalm 44:22). ***"Yet in all these things we are more than conquerors though Him who loved us.*** *For I am persuaded that neither death nor life, nor angels nor principalities nor powers, nor things present nor things to come, nor height nor depth, nor any other created thing, shall be able to separate us from the love of God which is in Christ Jesus our Lord."*

"As More Than Conquerors" We Walk In Our Identification with Christ in Whom We Died to Sin

In the middle of his resonating quotation is the statement. *"Yet in all these things we are more than conquerors though Him who loved us."* This reality in the Christian life is the epitome of our inheritance in Christ. Every provision for victory has been made for us; it comes to us in the Message of the Cross.

In the first Adam we were born **dead in sin,** in Christ we were born **dead to sin**--a world of difference. Our death to sin **was** a judicial death that honors the work that God himself did at the Cross. It is not our impossible task to die to sin; it is ours to accept in simple faith what God did once and for all in Christ. The work was done at the Cross; the struggle with our insufficient resources is over. It is now a faith and trust walk, a faith that commits and counts on the faithful ministry of the Holy Spirit whose strength is ours and on whom we draw in humble submission.

It is a process, a walk of maturing and growing in grace. Just as we were saved by an act of simple faith based on his death and resurrection without our works, so in the very same way--no difference--we accept our death in him and trust the Holy Spirit to do his work of renewing. We don't keep on asking forever for the Spirit's help; we take by faith what the Word gives us and where that simple faith exists the Spirit operates faithfully. It is a walk of faith and gratitude, a learning pattern.

Paul's personal testimony in Galatians can be ours in reality. "*I through the law died to the law* [that is, self-effort] *that I might live to God. I have been crucified with Christ; it is no longer I who live, but Christ lives in me; and the life which I now live in the flesh, I live by faith in the Son of God who loved me and gave Himself for me.*"

Charles Wesley immortalized the love of Christ in a hymn that we used to sing often:

And can it be that I should gain
An int'rest in the Savior's blood?
Died He for me who caused His pain?
For me, who Him to death pursued?
Amazing love! How can it be
that Thou, my God, shouldst died for me?

'Tis mystery all! The Immortal dies!
Who can explore His strange design?
In vain the first-born seraph tries
to sound the depths of love divine!
'Tis mercy all! Let earth adore,
Let angel minds inquire no more.

He left His Father's throne above,
So free, so infinite His grace;
Emptied Himself of all but love,
And bled and died for Adam's helpless race;
'Tis mercy all, immense and free;
For, O my God, it found out me.

Long my imprisoned spirit lay
Fast bound in sin and nature's night;
Thine eye diffused a quickening ray,
I woke, the dungeon flamed with light;
My chains fell off, my heart was free;
I rose, went forth, and followed Thee.

No condemnation now I dread;
Jesus, and all in Him, is mine!
Alive in Him, my living Head,
And clothed in righteousness divine.
Bold I approach the eternal throne,
And claim the crown, through Christ my own.

Charles Wesley (1707-1788)

It is no wonder that Paul after unveiling the glory of the **Grand Design,** the **Reign of Grace,** concludes the major section of Romans 1-11 with a matchless doxology equal to the greatest:

Oh, the depth of the riches both of the wisdom and knowledge of God!

How unsearchable are His judgments and His ways past finding out!

"For who has known the mind of the LORD? Or who has become His counselor?

"Or who has first given to Him and it shall be repaid to him?"

For of Him, and through Him and to Him are all things, To whom be glory forever. Amen."

A composite of Old Testament texts
--Isaiah 40:13, Jeremiah 23:18; Job 41:11;
with Hebrews 2:10; 13:21

About the Author

Gordon Ernest Johnson was born in Winnipeg, Manitoba, Canada, in a godly home. His mother, an Irish saint, was his first and lasting mentor. He attended Prairie Bible Institute High School in Three Hills, Alberta, Canada. In grade nine, 1942, he responded to God's call to prepare himself for lifelong missionary service in the first fall conference he attended.

During the following seven years, he sat under the godly influence of Rev. L. E. Maxwell, co-founder of Prairie, who became his second mentor. Gordon was an avid reader of the writings of Andrew Murray, Jessie Penn-Lewis, Keswick authors, L. E. Maxwell and Dr. F. J. Huegel, dean of missionaries to Mexico (1920-1970), who would become his third mentor.

During further education in Winnipeg, he took a pastorate where God humbled his heart and began to reveal the truths of the Cross. God sovereignly redirected the lives of Gordon and his wife, Grace, from Africa to Mexico and the Rio Grande Bible Institute in Edinburg, Texas.

In 1954 they set out for the Texas Mexican border in faith as did Abraham of old. With little promised financial support and two daughters, they would see God provide a lifelong teaching ministry that will soon reach 60 years.

The years of teaching Bible in Spanish and English (1954-2013) afforded him the privilege of sharing the truths of the Cross with thousands of alumni: Anglo career missionaries in the Spanish Language School and Hispanic young people in the Bible Institute. During his presidency (1981-1995) the

"Asociación de Exalumnos" was formed; he directed the yearly congresses throughout Mexico. He traveled with this message to 17 countries in Latin America.

In 2001, the Board of the school asked him to minister to the alumni. His former students had already become his burden: to see them understand and live the *Message of the Cross.* He began the writing of expository studies, brief, practical and centered in that precious truth. His target audience initially was Hispanic pastors, lay leaders and committed Christians in missionary service. The studies were sent by e mail.

In 2010 under the leadership of Dr. Larry Windle, RGBI formed Editorial Rio Grande, the publishing arm of the school. Using the latest in technology Editorial Rio Grande has published four of his books in **Spanish:** *Challenges from the Cross, Leadership from the Cross, Galatians--the Epistle of the Cross and the Spirit* and *Romans--Abundant Life in Union with Christ.*

The present expository study in Romans was written originally as bimonthly e mail studies, slightly enlarged and revised. I commend it to God's Spirit and his work of grace in your life.

About the Author

About Rio Grande Bible Institute

Rio Grande Bible Institute (RGBI) is an evangelical missionary organization that God has raised up to prepare workers for the Church in Latin America. It is fundamental in its doctrine and firmly believes in the verbal inspiration and the final authority of the Word of God. It seeks to serve all churches and denominations that share the same doctrine and practice.

The Rio Grande Bible Institute (RGBI) exists to glorify God by serving the Hispanic church through equipping leaders, edifying believers, and evangelizing the lost.

The primary campus is located in Edinburg, Texas, USA. The geographic area, called the Rio Grande Valley, is a broad plain of the Rio Grande River that constitutes the border between Texas and Mexico.

Rio Grande Bible Institute was founded by the Reverend M. C. Ehlert in 1946 with the purpose of training workers to evangelize the Rio Grande Valley. In those early years, there were two Bible schools, one in Spanish and one in English. In 1955 the leadership decided to close the English Bible school, and instead opened a language school to teach Spanish to missionaries who were preparing to serve in Latin America.

Over the years RGBI has been involved in numerous ministries. As the ministries developed and matured, many of them became independent daughter ministries. Some of the current ministries that are part of the Rio Grande Bible Institute include the four year accredited Spanish language Bible College, the Missionary Language School, and three radio stations, one AM and two FM. It also includes video production department that produces Bible courses for study by extension, a Bible Conference Center, and numerous other ministry ventures. God has prospered the faithful efforts greatly!

The Bible College portion of the ministry (called *Seminario Bíblico Río Grande*) exists to develop Christ-centered leaders with a Biblical worldview for the global church. It is a fully accredited bachelor's level school, and is authorized by the U.S. Government to enroll students from foreign countries. More than 6000 young people have studied in our schools.

The teaching staff consists of well-qualified teachers, both Latino and Anglo, with good academic preparation. They are united in the sacred call to invest their lives and future in training leaders for the Spanish-speaking church.

God sustains the Rio Grande Bible Institute through prayer and donations from His people. The ministry depends entirely upon this faith principle of dependence on God, and seeks to train all of its students to learn to do the same. The school staff and faculty members receive no fixed salaries, but rather depend entirely on the donations that are sent by the people of God. Due to this conviction, the Bible College education expenses are minimal. In light of the specific calling to serve the Latin American church, and in light of the huge economic disparity that plagues the Latin economies, this is a vital point. The vision of the school is to provide a strong Biblical preparation for those who have been called into ministry, even if they have few economic resources.

The College seeks to produce men and women who have been definitely impacted through its ministry; men and women who manifest Godly character and integrity; who know and handle the Word well; who demonstrate a solid doctrinal understanding and proficiency; who have an accurate and intimate knowledge of the world's needs and a vision for ministry; and who embrace a personal commitment to the task of making disciples of all nations.

The student who comes to the *Seminario Bíblico Río Grande* will find a school where the development of their spiritual life is considered to be the highest priority. Classes are greatly challenging academically, but the goal is always to produce obedience to the Word of God, and not mere intellectual knowledge. The course of study emphasizes the union of the believer with Christ and the impact of this in everyday Christian life. The leadership is designed and focused as a "service" to the Lord and to his Church, which is realized only by good preparation and the constant guidance of the Holy Spirit.

The student will also find a school that strongly challenges the trainee to be disciplined in the *use of their time*. The program of student work that links physical work together with the program of studies and the reality of coexisting with a myriad of new cultures, formed by the union of people from different places, and requires a tailored and unique discipline from the learner. The intensity of studies (with tasks, tests, and other academic responsibilities), practical service on weekends and work program combine to develop a discipline in the life of that student who seeks to have good testimony in everything he or she does. Graduates of the school greatly appreciate the discipline they learned during their stay here and comment that it has served them very well for a life of ministry.

The student will discover a school that strongly challenges the trainee to be *disciplined in his or her personal life*. The school believes that a minister of Christ must maintain an unblemished life and have high standards of behavior governing all that he or she does. Obedience and submission to God, even under difficult situations, are seen as crucial in the preparation for ministry. Standards and expectations will not always be the same as they were in the student's family or church, but no student should consider coming to the Bible College if he or she is not willing to obey and conform to the rules of the school as part of the "Basic-Training" that God has placed in their path of preparation for ministry.

For thousands of radio listeners in South Texas and northern Mexico, the Rio Grande Valley is the home of their favorite station, *Radio Esperanza*. This exciting AM and FM ministry (KRIO 910 AM, KOIR 88.5 FM, and KBMI 97.7 FM) beams the Gospel in Spanish into areas where missionaries or pastors may never be able to go. For those areas beyond the reach of the radio waves, Radio Esperanza is also available on the internet. Radio personnel also serve the Hispanic community by providing news and information about health, education, and job opportunities.

Our gracious God has given the Rio Grande Bible Institute a valuable tool for mass outreach, thus advancing the mission of the school in the following ways:

1. Reaching lost people
2. Providing support in the training of believers
3. Supporting local churches.

For a growing number of Latin American believers, Rio Grande is a source of excellent Bible study courses. *Video Esperanza* provides courses offered at Rio Grande Bible Institute, as well as other video and audio materials, to those who are unable to attend classes on the campus.

The materials are equally profitable for both the training of leaders in the local church and presentation to the general congregation.

For the *Winter Volunteers*--a special group of friends from the North who come to campus each winter--Rio Grande is a place to serve the Lord. These industrious volunteers have built most of the campus buildings, enabling the Institute to be better stewards of the finances God provides. Their contributions in a variety of areas, ranging from cooking to quilting and from landscaping to plumbing, are greatly appreciated by staff and students alike.

Winter Volunteers come from all parts of the U.S. and Canada to serve the Lord and share in the mission work of Rio Grande Bible Institute with their skills.

Bibleville is a non-denominational Bible Conference Center near Alamo, Texas, where "Winter Texans" share their faith and participate in varied activities from November through April.

A spacious 800-seat auditorium, palm-lined streets, Christian neighbors, and mission-centered activities make Bibleville an attractive and desirable place to spend the winter.

Editorial Rio Grande is the book publishing aspect of the ministry of Rio Grande Bible Institute. Using the latest in publishing technologies, Editorial Rio Grande employs on-demand book publishing and online marketing, as well as producing formats available for *Kindle, ebook,* and other digital means that will facilitate the easy dispersal of the products. Formal arrangements have been made to include some of the digital books in the Bible translation software packages provided to Bible translation groups, and in software packages that provide digital libraries for pastors, professors, and lay leaders across the world. God has enabled for the publication of some scholarly tools, such as a Hebrew/Spanish lexical concordance by Dr. George Parker, and a Biblical

Aramaic/Spanish grammar by Dr. Lewis Tyler. Editorial Rio Grande has been privileged to publish several deeper life books that detail the message of the Cross of Christ in the life of the believer, including *"Retos desde la Cruz," "Liderazgo desde la Cruz," "Galatas: La Epistola de la Cruz y el Espíritu Santo,"* and *"Romanos, la vida abundante en union con Cristo,"* by Dr. Gordon Johnson. This volume, *"Romans, the Reign of Grace in the Message of the Cross,"* is the first English language volume, but carries the same theme of the Cross as his other books. Editorial has also obtained the Spanish rights for all of Dr. F. J. Huegel's deeper life books, and currently includes *"Siempre triunfante"* (*"Forever Triumphant"*) and *"La cruz sin velos"* (*"The Cross Unveiled"*) in its roster of provisions. Immediate plans for future publications include an English volume on 2 Corinthians, an English volume on Colossians and a Spanish volume on Ephesians by Dr. Johnson; and continuing with the translation and publishing of Dr. Huegel's books.

As a person reflects on the faithfulness of God in creating the vision, supplying for the needs, and abundantly blessing RGBI with fruit since 1946, the words of Nehemiah 6:16 seem an appropriate reflection: "And it came to pass, that when all our enemies heard *thereof*, and all the heathen that *were* about us saw *these things*, they were much cast down in their own eyes: for they perceived that this work was *wrought of our God*!" If you have the opportunity to travel to the far south of Texas, come, see what God hath wrought!

--Dr. Lawrence B. Windle

CPSIA information can be obtained
at www.ICGtesting.com
Printed in the USA
FSOW02n0342280415
6707FS